Decline of Pakistan

Essays on federalism, ethnic-nationalism, minorities and human rights in Pakistan

By

Zulfiqar Shah

CreateSpace, An Amazone Company

Forewords

Unlike past decades, Pakistan is now a highly predictable and cognizable state, society and polity. It can only be appropriately analyzed through the deep understanding of ethnology of federalism; the conflict between state and society; colonial strings of internal exploitation, the divide and rule policy of the establishment; and finally through the futurologistic perception of the country by examining the matrix of climate change, land and politics. The book is a compilation of essays on Pakistan that give an ultimate outlook of the past, present and future of Pakistan. The essays were published in daily The Kathmandu Post, Nepal, daily Afghanistan Times, Kabul, Daily Dawn, Pakistan, Daily The News, Pakistan as well as on the websites of Truthout, USA, The Descrier, UK, CLAWS, India and Merinews, India.

Zulfiqar Shah

New Delhi, India
September 30, 2014
www.zulfiqarshah.com

CONTENTS

Ethnology of Federalism

State versus People

6

Colonial Strings of Internal Exploitation

Divide & Rule

Human Rights and Civil Liberties

Climate, Land & Politics

ETHNOLOGY OF FEDERALISM

Why Pakistan Is Not Changing

"Change" and "Pakistan" are the words of significant disconnect for Pakistanis and the world outside. The world outside has many illusions about Pakistan. The federation of the Indus civilizations' Muslim majority states is merely 70 years old, but houses a contemporary history of global geo-political engagements and is the epicenter of terror and violence in the name of Islam. It's also a hot spot for ethnic chauvinism that runs through the tectonic plates of the iron-clad military headquarters at Rawalpindi.

The vast majority of Pakistanis at home and abroad, as well as the stakeholder international community, have one common concern: why Pakistan is not changing for the better. A quest to seek answers needs a microcosmic reading of the ingredients and dynamism of change in Pakistan society vis-à-vis its state oligarchy and power matrix.

Class complexities

Pakistan has highly peculiar and complex traits of class formation, evolution and transformation, which have no match in the rest of the world in terms of social engineering by the state and its omni-powerful security establishment. During the period of Indian partition, Pakistan was predominantly a rural society comprised of mostly sharecroppers, peasants and landless agriculture laborers. It also had traditional feudal figures called Zamindars, who owned arable land traditionally, and feudal lords known as Jagirdars, who also held large amounts of arable land that was awarded to them by British colonizers in exchange for their loyalty and collaboration in British imperial endeavors in India. They were predominantly

Muslims. Despite three attempts between 1965 and 1978, no effective land reforms took place. The fear of socialist inroads led to Pakistan's establishment - with international support - gradually nationalizing emerging industry. Thus the process for the emergence of industrialists was barricaded. Led by the refugee feudal leadership of the ruling Muslim League and the Punjabi military, feudal lords were strengthened to cement the foundations of the military establishment in politics so that they might remain unchallenged, as urbanization and industrialization were the basis for change.

It is worth mentioning here that during the Indian partition of 1947, the Punjab Regiment of the undivided Indian Army was carved out to become the Pakistan Army. In the later phase of the military takeover of the state in Pakistan, despite leveling the playing field for the development of industrialists, the military itself turned its retired and serving officials into industrialists, thus creating a militarized industrialist and trading class. This ensured the status quo as well as a cushion for military-controlled change in Pakistan. Moreover, by facilitating the employment of state institutions for legitimate use of violence (police, second-tier military outfits like Pakistan Rangers, Frontier Constabulary and Bajwaur Wing) by the feudal loyalists in rural areas, and urban land grabbers, thugs, mafias, mullahs and terrorists in urban hubs like Karachi (Sindh), and to a certain extent in Quetta (Balochistan), Peshawar (Khyber Pakhtunkhuwa) and Lahore (Punjab), the security establishment created a "third state" to safeguard its interests. Thus, the elements of change were permanently resisted in Pakistan.

This resistance was further fueled and infected by the funded seminaries (Madrasas) preaching the Salafi brand of Islam among the majority Sunni Muslims of Pakistan, who were mostly Sufi by the cultural virtues of the Indus civilization. Hence, the mechanisms to transform Pakistan from rural and feudal into modern; from religious extremism of central Punjab and parts of South Punjab and Pashtun tribal areas into liberal; and urban mafias, thugs, and terrorists into change-monger city dwellers has been taken over by the military and its broader security establishment. Therefore, the shrinking of civil and liberal spaces in Pakistan has become phenomenal - despite the fact that the majority of the citizens in Pakistan that reside in the Sindh, Balochistan, South Punjab and Pashtun belt are either secular (as in the case of Sindh) or liberal. Consequently, talking about change in Pakistan means coining terms like "pro-civilians of the military" and "pro-military civilians." Maverick terms like "liberal extremists" are usually used by the extremist component of the Pakistani security establishment to describe the vocal Sindhi classes and socio-political elements.

Ethnicity faultlines

A broader ethnic diversity that could have become a vital motor for progress in Pakistan has now converted into the source of an ethnic divide and antagonism - mostly due to the military and security establishment's preference of some ethnic groups over the others. The unwritten constitution of the Pakistani establishment has one guiding principle - the dividing line between "hard-core" Pakistanis and second-, third- and fourth-level Pakistanis. Hence, trust and participation in statecraft has been prejudicial and exclusionary since the predominantly Punjabi security establishment buys the idea that of citizens belonging to any of the 11 Punjabi-speaking districts of Punjab province, religious Salafi/Wahabi or Sunni Muslims are the most trustworthy, hard-core Pakistanis. Urdu-speaking Indian partition refugees from northern India fall into the second "level"; the Hindko-speaking people from Hazara Division of Khyber Pakhtunkhuwa, the third; the Persian-speaking Hazara refugees from Afghanistan in Balochistan, fourth; and Salafi /Sunni Pashtuns are the fifth in the category of so-called "defined priority categorization" of "hard-core" Pakistanis.

This "prioritization" resulted in the inclusion of some ethnic groups in statecraft and the exclusion of others like Sindhi and Baloch, as well as Hindu, Christians, Shia and, to a certain extent, Ahmadis, creating the foundations for ethnic conflict, interest strife, freedom movements and warfare in Pakistan. This matrix of conflict may be categorized as Sindhi, Baloch and Pashtun versus the Punjabi-dominated establishment. It can also be categorized as a competition over participation in governance and access to resources between Baloch and Hazara refugees in Balochistan; Sindhi and Urdu-speaking Sindhis in Sindh and Pashtun and the Hindko-speaking communities in Khyber Pakhtunkhuwa; and between Siraki, Potohari and Punjabi in Punjab. This dynamic has been created in the first instance and is now utilized for furthering the Punjabi-dominated establishment. Eventually, the phenomena has created a Bangladesh (previously East Pakistan)-like situation in Sindh and Balochistan.

A State of anarchy

Anarchy has engulfed the Pakistani state apparatus. The conflict between the civilian population and noncivilians is at center stage. The former includes the pro-civilian fold, the upholders of civilian dominance in statecraft in the form of political parties: social groups, dissenter individuals and pro-civilian elements. The pro-military fold includes serving and retired armed forces personnel and the military-associated intelligence fraternity, pro-military elements within the political parties and civil bureaucracy and parts of civil society.

Moreover, two groups are crosscutting elements in Pakistan - military and mullah. They have inroads into almost all social groups and schools of thought of the state and society, with the only low-scale "infected elements," the larger majority of activists in Sindh and Balochistan who strive for freedom or secession. This great puzzle of state and society in the South Asia of our times is a predecessor of the ongoing and upcoming worst form of anarchy in the state and the society among the federations of the world.

Road to change

Achieving positive change in Pakistan would be like an attempt to wash the dirt out from a cowboy's jeans. In the context of socio-economic complexities, political traits and the ethno-religious composition of the military-dominated state apparatus and establishment of Pakistan, there would be some necessary prerequisites. Changing the ethno-religious composition of all civil, military and security governance segments of the state would be a primary requirement. Cutting off the nexus between feudal and urban lords and the criminal security regime of the country - misused for the manipulation of society and polity in favor of military interests - would be necessary. That would also lead to an ultimate shutdown of religious-terrorist factories in Punjab. It is important to de-Punjabize the state apparatus and reduce the existence of Hindko, Urdu and Hazara ethnic minorities, proportionate to their civilian population, however, it is worth mentioning here that the Shia Hazara of Balochistan are also the worst victims of state-sponsored Salafi terrorism.

The change in the ethnic composition of Pakistan's military is the unavoidable prerequisite, given that Sindhis are almost nonexistent in the Sindh Regiment, Baloch in the Baloch Regiment, and Siraki in the Punjab Regiment. The same is evident in the technical corps and specialized formations of the military. Surprisingly, the residents of coastal Sindh and Balochistan are not part of the Naval Forces, and inhabitants of high-altitude Mountains are nonexistent in the Air Force. Moreover, the hegemony of Punjab in the Parliament needs to be altered. According to the arrangements under the 1973 constitution of Pakistan, Sindh, Balochistan and Khyber Pakhtunkhuwa provinces together do not form a numerical two-third majority in the parliament to amend the constitution of Pakistan. If desired, the Punjab, in association with its collaborating ethnic minorities, can amend and legislate the constitution. In such a situation, religious extremist Punjabi-speaking Punjabi, eyeing Afghanistan and the Indian Kashmir, can never be willing to undo the Jihadi machinery and repeal notorious laws like the blasphemy law, as well as arrangements that bar Non-Muslims from holding the offices of president, prime minister and armed forces chiefs.

Moreover, the preamble to the Constitution of Pakistan should be excluded, as it was, in fact, a resolution by the All India Muslim League's central working committee to turn Pakistan into an Islamic Republic after the death of Jinnah. If these changes are not made, the existence of Pakistan will be disastrous for its own victimized majority of the people in Sindh, Balochistan, Khyber Pakhtunkhuwa and Siraikistan (South Punjab) and pose a danger of greater anarchy and instability in South Asia and the Central Asian region. There are only two options for Pakistan, according to the realities of our times: Exist after undertaking wider drastic reforms or vanish by dividing into two or three new sovereign countries on the world map. There is no middle path.

Published on Truthout, USA on April 05, 2014

Federalism in Pakistan

Federalism in South Asia has many forms. Pakistan, Sri Lanka and Afghanistan have remained highly volatile federations in post-colonial South Asia; whereas, India, the largest democracy as well as one of the largest federations on the globe, has its own dynamics. Federal practices are being revisited everywhere in the region–reconstruction in Afghanistan, revisions in Pakistan, restructuring in Sri Lanka, constitutional process in Nepal, rethinking over Chittagong in Bangladesh and over Kurdistan and Sistan in Iran.

Pakistan is the only South Asian country which been broken in the post-colonial period and is once again under the same threat; therefore it is important to learn from its federal practices, particularly in relation to Sindh, now a province but which was a sovereign country for over 2,000 years until the British set foot in 1843. It not only voluntarily chose to become a part of Pakistan in 1947 but also gave birth to Mohammad Ali Jinnah, the country's Pakistan.

Pakistan is a peculiar federalism with two permanent, conflicting features, which act as foundations of its federal crises. The country runs eight administrative units but looks to secure the interests of only one ethnicity at the cost of others.

The provinces of Sindh and Punjab are almost modern democracies. Balochistan is a tribal administration. Khyber Pakhtunkhuwa (formerly NWFP) has four administrative systems where major cities are modern democracies and the rest is divided into Federally Administered Tribal Areas (FATA), Federal Criminal Regulation Area (FCR or semi tribal areas) and Shariat Law for Mehemend Agency.

This permanent diversity is in keeping with the aspirations of people from different backgrounds; however it was not appropriately reviewed until last year, when FATA was constitutionally given the rights of electoral franchise and political association.

The other permanent feature of federalism in the country is political and legislative arrangements securing dominating majority and economic prosperity of Punjab province over the rest, in what people from other provinces term demographic hegemony. The history of state-building and legislation in Pakistan, basically, revolves around this single factor.

During the partition of India, the majority of All India Muslim League (AIML) supporters from Muslim minority provinces in northern and central India migrated to Pakistan. They were heartily welcomed by Sindhi people. Muhajirs (refugees), as they called themselves, were settled in selective urban hubs of Sindh including Karachi, Hyderabad and Sukkur so as to create constituencies for the immigrant AIML leaders. Therefore ALML leadership favored non-democratic politics.

In 1958, General Ayub Khan took over with the help of civil bureaucracy and AIML leadership and gave the country its first comprehensive constitution. This was followed by the imposition of 'One Unit System' on the basis of parity between eastern and western wings of Pakistan. The East Pakistan Bengalis were a majority in the newly formed Pakistan; therefore, they were countered through the merger of Punjab, Sindh, Balochistan and NWFP into single province of West Pakistan against the will of three latter provinces.

Publishing, reading and writing in Sindhi language was banned during One Unit because Sindhi was the only language in Pakistan which had a script and was the language of academia. Urdu was imposed as a national language, which was resisted by Sindhis and Bengalis. Finally, One Unit had to be abolished due to fear of liberation movement in Bangladesh.

Pakistan was given its third constitution in 1973 by PM Minister Zulfiqar Ali Bhutto who hailed from Sindh. This time, the principle of majority democracy was adopted which suited demographic majority of Punjab. Later on, Bhutto was executed under general Zia's martial law imposed in 1977, which led Sindh into a decade-long resistance that was countered through a five-pronged strategy of militarization; criminalization through dacoits; creating tribal fiefdoms in non-tribal Sindh districts; encouraging ethnic violence by Muhajirs in Karachi and Hyderabad; and managing demographic influx of Afghan refugees and Punjabis to Sindh. At one stage during this process, the military was transformed into a separate interest group, and the political process of 1990's in Pakistan was basically marked by conflict between civilian and non-civilian actors.

The post 9/11 Pakistani federalism attempts a viable statehood. But the genesis of separatism are still there, as was evident in the Dec 27, 2007 assassination of Benazir Bhutto, when Pakistan ceased to exist in Sindh for three days and nights; however, mass uprising were soon overpowered by Asif Zardari, husband and political successor of Benazir Bhutto. Sindh and Balochistan today are strongholds of freedom movements. Murders of Sindhi nationalist leaders and enforced disappearances of hundreds of political and rights activists has become a routine.

Sindh's experience with federalism offers some important lessons. Only a federalism that offers political pluralism and ethnic as well as demographic securities can have permanence. Federation entails just distribution of resources, right to rule, maintaining demographic majority and appropriate share in all forms of statecraft and power in historic land. If a federation develops a foreign policy without accommodating people's and especially federating states' will, the consequences can be disastrous.

South Asian countries' varied experiences in federalism can be shared to each country's benefit, including Nepal.

Identities are also important in single-nation countries, although of an entirely different nature. In Nepal and Bangladesh districts or divisions are administrative provinces, therefore their development and economic viability is a matter of high importance. In case of disagreement, mediation, consultation and understanding between conflicting administrative units are the solution. One of the long-running disputes in Sindh over the division of Larkana district was resolved when the newly formed district of Shahdadkot was jointly named 'Qambar-Shahdadkot' after mediation.

South Asian countries have versatile experiences of federal practices and we can share them for each other's benefits. Why not facilitate this through establishment of a South Asian Court of Justice and South Asian Forum of Federating States under SAARC or any other arrangement? Such a body can help devise conflict resolution mechanisms and by doing so eliminate the chances of violence, dismemberments and political conflicts in federations of South Asia.

There are many conflicts within federations in Africa, resolution of which would be a milestone towards, peace, development and human security. In fact, the United Nations could be a legitimate forum for this, but it gives legitimate mandate only to sovereign countries, whereas the unresolved issues among federating states or between center and federating state are almost non-addressable in the forum. Thus restructuring of the United Nations in which federating states may be given legitimate space for reconciliation and resolution of disputes is urgently needed.

Published in Daily Republica, Kathmandu, Nepal on June 28, 2012

Political Economy of Federalism in Pakistan & Movement for

Self-Determination in Sindh

Pakistan is at a crossroads, its federal structure severely threatened by provincial independence movements fueled by ethnic tensions, structural political failures and the allocation of tax revenues.

Pakistan is on the brink again after 1971. Intensive decade-long secessionist warfare is underway in Balochistan, and a mass movement, accompanied by low-scale insurgency, has arisen in Sindh, which cast the shadow of popular uprising in March 2012, when hundreds of thousands took to the streets in the provincial capital Karachi, demanding independence for Sindh. Immediately after that "freedom march" in Karachi, its organizer, and popular freedom movement leader Bashir Qureshi, died under mysterious circumstances. It is widely believed in Sindh that he was poisoned by the security agencies of Pakistan. This concern of the Sindhi people has been validated by the medical investigations report carried out by a medical board formed by the Sindh Health Department and confirmed by the then-home minister of Sindh, Manzoor Wasan, in an interview by a Sindhi daily, Awami Awaz, in Karachi.

Qureshi's demise was followed by the murder of another resistance movement leader, Muzaffar Bhutto, who was forcedly disappeared in 2011 at the hands of security agencies, according to the various international and Pakistani human rights bodies. Another brutal act was previously reported in April 2011, when three freedom movement leaders were burned alive by the security agencies in the Sanghar district of Sindh, according to a fact-finding report of the Human Rights Commission of Pakistan. Several hundred people are still illegally detained or disappeared across the province.

The popular uprising in Sindh is meaningful because the province contributes a large share to Pakistan's economy and is the second largest province, home to over 50.54 million people. Moreover, it is the only state that voluntarily became part of Pakistan by adopting the Pakistan Resolution in the Sindh Legislative Assembly in 1946. M.A. Jinnah, founder of the country, was an ethnic Sindhi and died due to health-care negligence by the country's second line leadership; three ethnic Sindhi prime ministers of Pakistan were illegally dismissed from office by the military during their five terms of government, and two of them were killed in Punjab province. Zulfiqar Ali Bhutto was executed under General Zia al Haq's martial law, which is commonly termed judicial murder in Pakistan, and his daughter Benazir Bhutto was assassinated in the backyard of the military's General Headquarters in Rawlapindi during General Musharaf's rule in 2007. It is academically well documented by Stephen P. Cohen in his book The Pakistan Army that the armed forces in Pakistan contain an overwhelming ethnic Punjabi majority.

Economic and fiscal Exploitation

Sindh has contributed a significant 32.7 percent historical average to Pakistan's GDP; meanwhile, the provinces' own GDP per capita is $1,400. Fifteen percent of Sindh's GDP is lost due to environmental degradation caused mostly by Punjab's water rights violations as well as by faulty drainage schemes carrying industrial and agricultural waste through Sindh from the higher elevation province of Punjab.

According to the Pakistan Energy Book 2007, an estimated 1,000,415 MMcf (million cubic feet) of natural gas is produced in Sindh, which accounts for 70.77 percent of Pakistan's total gas production; Sindh produces 13.87 million barrels of oil, which is 56.36 percent of Pakistan's total oil production. Oil extracted from Sindh had an annual value of $1.75 billion, out of which the province's financial receipts were 12.5 percent, and the employment share was below 1 percent for ethnic Sindhis. In June 2011, the elected parliament in Pakistan, through the 18th constitutional amendment, transferred authority over the country's natural resources to the provinces that improved the financial share in their own resources, however the amendment has not yet been implemented, and the authority to negotiate exploration of coal reservoirs in Sindh has been unlawfully handed over to the federal government. It is worth mentioning that unearthed coal reserves in Sindh total 175 billion tons.

Pakistan first explored its natural gas reservoirs in Balochistan during the 1950s, but the province could only utilize those resources for its own residents after 1986, when an armed forces cantonment was established in Quetta, capital of the province. In the past 65 years, only 7 percent of this resource has been utilized by the residents of the Balochistan. Until 2008, Sindh consumed 45 percent of its gas production, while Punjab consumed 930 percent of its total gas production. Despite their highest shares of the natural resources of Pakistan, Sindh and Balochistan are kept out of the development mainstream. This is validated by the Millennium Development Goals Report of 2005 issued by the government of Pakistan, which mentions that the oil-, gas- and coal-rich districts of Sindh and Baluchistan had poor indicators of human development. An estimated 76 percent of Pakistan's known oil reserves are located in Sindh, but extremely centralized economic and fiscal federalism has given birth to the conflict between the province and the center.

The National Finance Commission (NFC) is the federal fiscal structure, where revenue collected by the provinces is pooled and distributed to the federal and provincial governments every five years. Such a periodic revenue distribution is called an "NFC Award" in Pakistan and has been practiced since 1971. In 1991, provinces received 20 percent and the center 80 percent of the country's total tax revenue, a proportion reformed in 1997, with 37 percent for the provinces and 63 percent for the center. In 1997, Sindh contributed 65 percent, Punjab 25 percent, Khyber Pakhtunkhuwa 7 percent and Balochistan 3 percent of the country's tax revenues; however Sindh received 9 percent of the redistributed revenues, Punjab 25 percent, Khyber Pakhtunkhwa 6 percent and Balochistan received 2 percent, while the rest went to the central government. Until 1997, the resource distribution was made on the basis of population, which gave an ultimate edge to the Punjab - which accounts for 60 percent of the country's total population.

The most recent NFC Award of 2010 was further reformed promising a 57.5 percent share of revenues to the provinces and a 42.5 percent share to the center in 2011. Other factors of distribution given weight along with population were also included. For example, now population accounts for 82 percent of the weighting; poverty, 10.3 percent; revenue generation, 5 percent; and inverse population density, 2.7 percent. Sindh is the greatest loser in this reform, as despite being the major revenue generator, Sindh receives 24.5 percent; meanwhile Punjab receives 51.7 percent as its receipts remain unchallenged because of population; Khyber Pakhtunkhuwa and Balochistan remained reasonable well-taken care of, receiving 14.6 percent and 9.11 percent, respectively, out of the total share of the provinces.

Punjab has a dual economic and fiscal edge - the 82 percent share in the fiscal distribution among the provinces and another major share through the federal civil and military departments – gained primarily from the ethnic Punjabi majority. According to the 2012-13 budget, 18.4 percent of Pakistan's budget is allocated for the defense, which is higher than any of the civilian budget rubrics for the country, especially because, when combined with overall security expenditures, including the defense, interior and strategic departments, it will amount to at least an estimated 30 percent of the country's total budget. The ethnic composition of the key security organs - including the ministry of defense, ministry of foreign affairs and interior ministry, along with the armed forces, second-tier armed institutions and law enforcing agencies - is overwhelmingly Punjabi, which ultimately means that the economic flow derived from federal government employment opportunities, procurement and other expenditures is also directed toward Punjab.

Politics of underdevelopment

According to a poverty assessment in Sindh by Asian Development Bank (ADB) in 2008, due to a growing population and a rise in literacy and migration, nearly 600,000 additional people will be entering the job market each year in Sindh. This is in contrast to the long-term annual job creation rate of 350,000 in the province.

Agro-based industry could provide some relief, but poor law-and-order conditions and weak infrastructure has been a barrier. Industry in Sindh is mainly concentrated in Karachi, except for a handful of units in Hyderabad, Kotri and Sukkur. Until 2008, about 11,500 industrial units were located in Karachi, the capital of Sindh, employing 2.5 million people, but the share of ethnic Sindhi people remained less than 10 percent. That compares poorly to the strength of 45 technical institutions of Sindh in 2008, which registered 18,000 students, out of which 40 percent were from outside Karachi.

Though Karachi is the capital, the admission of students from the rest of the province into the public academic institutions is prohibited due to the legislation passed by the Mutahida Qaumi Movement (MQM)-led government in Sindh during the military rule of General Pervez Musharaf. Constitutionally, the chief minister is the province authority over the higher education institutions, but in Sindh, the governor of the province is the decision maker. A governor in Pakistan is a ceremonious representative of the federation in the provinces. The current governor, who has held the post the last 11 years, belongs to MQM, a Karachi-based ethnic (racial) outfit.

Basically, human resource development initiatives providing equal opportunity are required to create a socio-economic balance between urban and rural areas as well as between Sindh and Punjab.

Sindh has become a microcosm of the climate change. An erratic flow of the Indus River, which brings mega floods once in a while after many years of drought, disastrously aggravates poverty, unemployment and job insecurity.

The Indus flood of 2010 and rain floods of 2011 have intensified the vulnerability of a majority in Sindh. According to the Sindh government, the flood of 2010 wreaked havoc with Sindh by displacing 7.254 million people from 11,992 villages, inundating ripened crops on 24.821 million acres of land and destroying 876,000 houses. The losses for Sindh amount to $1.44 billion in agriculture, $0.12 billion in livestock, $1.42 billion in housing, $380 million in road infrastructure, 550 million in irrigation infrastructure, $41.5 million in health infrastructure, $32.5 million in educational infrastructure, $420 million in urban infrastructure and $100.6 million in the government building damages. Meanwhile, during the rain floods of 2011, around 8.9 million people were displaced, 152 million houses damaged and 6.77 million acres crops devastated. The losses from the 2011 floods were higher than those from the flood of 2010.

Water conflict

The major political struggles in Sindh after 1988 have focused on water shortages in Sindh and some mega irrigation projects like the Kalabagh Dam. The river water shortage has left its adverse effects on the ecological order of Sindh, agriculture, rural economy and culture.

The Indus Delta faces degradation threats. During the past two decades, the sea intrusion has resulted in tidal erosion and salt water intrusion of about 2.2 million acres of land in the Badin and Thatta districts in coastal Sindh, while mangrove forest cover has decreased from about 228,812 hectares to 73,001 hectares. Mangroves provide fuel wood to 1.2 million people, forage to 16,000 camels, and other products to 28,570 households and they shelter inland areas from coastal flooding.

Mangroves act as a shield against active tidal erosion in the area and support thousands of botanical, aquatic and wildlife species and provide a nursery for most of the 44 commercial fish and shrimp species in the deltaic area. All these benefits are dependent on the survival of the mangrove forest, which in turn needs freshwater flow in the estuaries. Unfortunately, the active delta is now only 10 percent of its original area. Sindh requires a minimum of 35 MAF (million acre feet) of water a year for its ecological sustenance and agricultural pursuits. The economic loss due to the Indus Delta devastation is estimated around $120 million annually, which does not include the unquantifiable value of environmental aspects such as biodiversity, habitat and coastal protection.

Demographic sovereignty

The peopling of Sindh began with the birth of Pakistan in 1947. It has now become a multiethnic and linguistic province due to migrations from within Pakistan and outside, altering the demographic fabric of its urban hubs. The census in Pakistan has not taken place since 1998. If demographic estimates are carried out today on the basis of 1998 census by including urban-rural and inter-provincial population shifts as well as external migration patterns in the context of broader ethno-linguist groups' context, the result would be: Sindhis 68 percent; Muhajirs (refugees) 19 percent and rest 17 percent. Muhajirs is a broader category in Sindh that includes Urdu-speaking refugees from India who migrated during the partition of the subcontinent in 1947 and non-Urdu and non-Sindhi Biharis, Guajarati, Rajasthanis, Bengalis and others who migrated from India, Bangladesh and elsewhere in South Asia after 1947. Similarly, in Karachi city, indigenous Sindhi and Sindhi of Balochi, Gujarati and Rajasthani origin comprise around 50 percent of the population; the Urdu-speaking of Indian origin and ethno-linguist Biharis of Bangladeshi origin are below 25 percent and the rest are 25 percent.

The existing political arrangements have threatened the demographic security and sovereignty of Sindhi people in their historic land due to nonexistence of legal and legislative frameworks. Neither the provincial legislature nor the government in Pakistan has first generation migrants or refugees as parliamentarians and ministers. It is in Sindh alone where first generation Punjabi and Pashtun migrants and refugees are both part of parliament and of the cabinet of the provincial government. The movement for demographic security in Sindh is as old as Pakistan itself, but the federation is unwilling to carry such legislation. Besides, federalism in Pakistan essentially enshrines Punjabi dominance, by which the federal legislative parliament contains an overwhelming majority of ethnic Punjabis, rather than a mix of Sindhis, Baloch and Pashtuns. Together, the later three do not form the obligatory two-thirds majority to legislate.

What is to be done?

Pakistan is again at a crossroads, as the reasons that led to the breakup of the country in 1971 exist today with more intensity for the oppressed provinces of Sindh, Balochistan and Pakhtunkhuwa. Essentially, the country requires major reforms of federalism that offer demographic, ethnic, economic, and fiscal as well as development security - and the consequent abolition of the ethnic hegemony of Punjab and its allies. Until federal reforms, combining proportionate representation and the participation of various provinces is ensured in all forms of statecraft, the freedom movement in Sindh will not only be well-justified, but also the only way out for the poor and marginalized 50 million people of this richest province of Pakistan.

Published in Truthout, USA on June 07 2013

Pakistan: Politics of Fallacies

External perceptions of Pakistani politics and society are often fallacious. The analysis, policies, and decisions based on these perceptions, assumptions, and myths regarding Pakistan in the outer world are therefore often fruitless. Whilst the fallacies are numerous, by following BuzzFeed's lead and producing a top ten list a picture begins to emerge.

Demographic majority

There is a much touted fallacy that Punjabi is the demographic majority in Pakistan, but the demographic majority of Punjab and Punjabis are two different things. Out of 34 districts of Punjab, 14 are Siraki speaking, four are Potoharis, and the other 18 are Punjabi speaking majority districts. Therefore, Punjabi are a simple majority in Punjab and not an overwhelming majority of Pakistan per se; however these 18 district dominate and control whole Pakistan and its state and non-state institutions civil and military institutions.

Sindh syndrome

It is widely believed in Pakistan and abroad that Urdu speaking (1947 refugees that identify themselves as Muhajirs) are a majority ethnic group of Sindh, meanwhile some have notion that they form majority in the Karachi city. Such a tactical data manipulations of 'demographic fallacies' are created to underestimate the real Sindhi population, because Sindh has been dissenting Pakistani federalism and foreign policies since 1948.

According to the census of Pakistan in 1998, the population of Sindh was 30.44 million. The ethnic break-up mentions in the census document that Urdu speaking were 18 percent out of it, which means in 1998 they were 5.479 million. Mutahida Qaumi Movement (MQM), the claimant of sole representative of Urdu speaking Sindhis (the claim itself is another fallacy), used to say that Urdu speaking people are a majority in Karachi, Hyderabad Sukkur, Mirpurkhas and Nawabshah. The total population of these cities, if combined according to the census of 1998, is 14.36 million. This means that Urdu-speaking Sindhis (Muhajirs) do not form majority in any city of Sindh or Pakistan.

Khaki truth

The majority of the military generals in the Pakistan Army since 1947 have been the first or the second generation of those Punjabi and Urdu-speaking refugees who migrated from India during and after the partition of 1947, and this is a major reason that the Pakistan Army has never pushed for a real democracy. Moreover, Pakistan's concept of security is based on geography rather than the population, which has resulted in the hatred of 1947 holding back any new India-Pakistan peace initiatives.

Islam and the republic

The constitution of the Republic mentions that the country is an Islamic Republic. However, as the history tells, Pakistan has been involved in the persecution of millions of Bengali, Baloch, Sindhi, and Pashtun Muslims in East Pakistan (now Bangladesh), Sindh, Balochistan, Khyber Pakhtunkhuwa and Afghanistan in the name of Islam. Becoming an "Islamic Republic" and acting in Islam's true and original sprit are two different things.

Civil democracy

The six-decade long process of the direct or indirect military rule in Pakistan has largely militarized almost all civil departments of the government, and majority of the non-government civil institutions in terms of their culture and loyalty to the supremacy of the military. There is, therefore, no 'civil' or 'civilian' socio-political and economic leadership in the contemporary Pakistan. There are only two things: civil of the military or militarized civilian leadership. However, those who have long dissented against the military establishment or opposed the very existence of Pakistan as a country (secessionist are mostly Sindhi and Baloch) have remained out of this course of militarization of the broader civilian fold.

Salafism and religious politics

Majority of the religious-political parties of Pakistan are indoctrinated with Salafi / Wahabi school of thought, but the majority population in Pakistan is Sunni-Hanfiya Muslim. Paradoxically, the Wahabi parties are representing Sunni majority Muslims, meanwhile leadership of Sunni organizations, according to media reports, prey victim of targeted killings in Karachi and Lahore. It is the real fault-line of the religious and sectarian terrorism and violence in Pakistan.

The status of the Taliban

The Pakistani Taliban has never been and can never be the independent elements or non-state actors. They are the proxy military of Pakistan, which misusing Islamic ideology are conducting warfare and violence for the strategic interests of their masters.

The Hindus population

Most of the columnists inside and outside Pakistan quote that Hindu population in Pakistan is merely two percent, which is one of the grand fallacies about Pakistan. Hindus, in fact, are more than 5.5 percent of Pakistan. The Hindus of Sindh form roughly 5 percent of Pakistan's total population. The problem with the official figures lies in the questions of the census, in which Hindus and Shudras (untouchables) are counted separately. The Hindus of Sindh, South Punjab, Balochistan and a small number in Khyber Pakhtunkhuwa together make up more than 5.5 percent of the population of Pakistan.

Political tagging of feudalism

According to census reports, the large number of TV, Radio and Satellite facility holders are Sindhi households. Sindhi and Sindhi of Baloch origin today form nearly 50 percent of Karachi, beyond 60 percent of Hyderabad and more than 70 percent of Sukkur as well as around 90 percent of Mirpurkhas, Nawabshah and Larkana cities. If seen in that context, Sindhis are largest urbanized population of Sindh; however, they are new urbanites in comparison with the large number of Urdu speaking Muhajirs, Biharis, Bengalis, and Gujaratis in terms of period of urbanization.

Due to these fallacies, the perception about Pakistan has been giving a different glimpse to the world outside. It is the only reason that most of the international analysts and experts on Pakistan do not predict the situations appropriately. Besides, this is the propagated manipulation, which non-representative Pakistani establishment has been doing internationally to secure it long terms single ethnic interests.

Published on The Descrier, UK on September 22, 2013

The Centre Cannot Hold

Federations around the world have adapted political systems to the foundations of their socio-political and cultural realities so that proclamations of identity, the trickling down of the fruits of governance to the grassroots level and the unfurling of even patterns of development based on parity become a tangible reality.

Two federations around the world—Pakistan and the US—are peculiar examples of federal systems with a relatively very short history of nation-making and statehood. Both of these countries were never a sovereign homogeneous state before becoming republics. However, they are polar opposites in terms of federalism and the sovereign autonomy of the federated states. Unlike the US, Pakistan has an extremely centralized political system, which, despite being a federation constitutionally, is a unitary form of governance in practical terms. Although it has reached the highly mature age of sixty-five years after waging three direct and two proxy wars on the Indian and Afghanistan borders, Pakistan has not learned lessons from its own history. The bitter realities of federalism, the political system and state-building have always created a political ecology unsuitable for the strengthening of substantive democracy in Pakistan.

Art of unitary federalism

Pakistan's democratic system is a microcosm of its federalism. Pakistan emerged from the 1940 resolution adopted by the All India Muslim League, which demanded the creation of a country consisting of the Muslim majority states of undivided India and ensuring maximum autonomy and sovereignty to the federated states. This was in reaction to the British India Act (the constitution) of 1935, which created a highly centralized political system. A few weeks after the creation of Pakistan, the very basis for the country was negated by the dissolving of an elected legislative assembly and the government in Pakhtunkhuwa, followed by the dissolution of the Sindh assembly and government. The 'sovereign states' of undivided India, which were independent countries before the British invasion, were downgraded to the status of provinces, going against the spirit of the 1940 resolution. Later on, in 1951, the status of provinces was undone and a unitary province of West Pakistan was created to counter the demographic majority of Bengal, which was East Pakistan. Education, writing, publishing and printing in Sindhi and Bengali languages were banned. Pakistan adopted a unitary political system in the name of 'parity federalism' under the shadow of the country's first military rule of General Ayub Khan. This was ultimately meant to keep Bengalis out of power despite being the demographic majority so that the interests of the East Pakistani majority ethnic group, the Punjabis, an overwhelming majority in the military, could be protected. After the break-up of Pakistan in 1971 under the second military rule of General Yahya Khan, a new constitution was adopted, which turned the country into a virtual unitary system based on the democratic monopoly of the ethnic majority of Punjabis. Even today, 65 years after Pakistan's creation, the seats of the Sindh, Balochistan and Pakhtunkhuwa provinces together do not form a two-thirds majority in the federal legislature, which means they cannot legislate according to their will against the vast share of the Punjab in the federal parliament.

Political ecology of democracy

The democratic system in Pakistan has hidden strings of demographic interest as well as numerical contours. It doesn't offer equal space to the ethnicities of the federated provinces and neither does it translate governance into qualitative democracy. A democratically elected government has never been given space to decide the country's foreign policy or make political interventions for sustainable internal security and development.

Human engineering within the political culture of the country was always aimed at upholding the rite of the omnipresent security establishment. Issues like the freedom movements in Sindh and Balochistan, which could only be resolved through political dialogue and engagement by ensuring more federalism, were left to the decisions of the trigger-happy security regime, which always preferred an eyeball-to-eyeball stance against dissenters to crush it through militarization.

Unfortunately, the domination of the security paradigm of statecraft over development has shrunk the quality of life and socio-economic growth of the common people, particularly in Sindh, Balochistan and Pakhtunkhuwa. The process has converted Pakistan into a security state, where the unwritten constitution outlines privileged ethnic groups like Punjabis and the Urdu community and Islamic schools of thoughts like Salafism and Devband as the core patriotic demography. This has given an edge to these ethnic and sectarian groups in statecraft and internal and external policies and has resulted in unending conflicts along the Afghanistan and Indian borders, promoted the Talbanization of Pakistan and secessionism in the Sindh and Balochistan provinces.

Statecraft of fragmentation and militarization

As an all-time military republic, statecraft in Pakistan has always tried to fragment, divert and pervert social ethos, cultural composition and political discourse. The chronic ailments of Pakistani society, bearers of the historical secular traits of the Indus civilization, are fanaticism and radical Islamization, tribal fiefdoms and feudalism, as well as ethnic chauvinism and the fascism of those dominating the state apparatus. These are the outcomes of the divide-and-rule policy of the military establishment, which preferred unitary federalism, non-substantive democracy and the ethno-sectarian monotony of the state apparatus.

Social and state fragmentation in Pakistan is the result of the decades' long practice of the upholding grip of non-civil actors so that the interests of privileged ethnic groups and the non-civil class, which has emerged in Pakistan as a separate social entity, are ensured, protected and furthered. This has led Pakistan to the militarization of society and civil spaces.

Possibilities and the pathway

As a result, Pakistan is swamped with fragmentation, chaos and anarchy. It is trying to fight issues of political, state and social chemistry in conventional and naïve ways. The failure of the political system is deeply rooted in its deviation from its foundations, which were the socio-cultural ethos of the Indus civilization and the spirit of the 1940 resolution. In the blind alley of state failure and socio-political anarchy, it has to choose one nation over the much abated two-nation theory. The adaptation of the latter has already resulted in the break-up of the country. It also has to shape a substantive democratic system, provide maximum autonomy and sovereignty to the federated states, undo the militarization of the Pakistani state and finally de-Talibanize Pakistani society.

Published in daily Kathmandu Post, Nepal on May 2, 2013

Towards One Southasia

Pakistani Prime Minister Nawaz Sharif, like ex-president Asif Ali Zardari, has recently tuned up the good old mantra of a visa-free India-Pakistan. However, the nature of geopolitical relations between these two countries alone is the major hurdle to a visa-free regime in the region. Given the fact that visa arrangements and norms between the rest of the Southasian countries are almost on the verge of border-free regional entities, it is speculated that a visa-and-border-free Southasia can only be realized, unlike the European Union, through a gradual visa-and-border regime change.

Southasian contours

Since Pakistani state behavior towards India has been of an infiltrative and offensive mode when it comes to peace and security, the reaction from India has been inevitable, although mild most of the time. It is therefore necessary to envision a paradigm shift in the Southasian visa regime, particularly between India and Pakistan. This requires out-of-the-box thinking around state apparatus, ethnic diversity, economic stability, demographic sovereignty and security, as well as the handling of intra-state conflicts, which in most countries has remained militaristic.

Nepal is still struggling to shaping an appropriate statehood. Sri Lanka has yet to build a social contract between the Sinhala and Tamil people. Bhutan has to think on the violence around Buddhism. India has to deepen its federal practices by addressing issues in Kashmir as well as in its northeastern parts. Pakistan has to alter the web of statehood, federalism and dismantle ethnic Punjabi hegemony on Sindh, Balochistan and Khyber Pakhtunkhuwa.

Pakistan, by all aspects, is not only a peculiar state in Southasia but also a must review case study among the federations of the globe, where ethno-sectarian monotony, ethnically exclusive statehood and state ideology stereotype has turned Pakistan into steadily failing state.

Dismantling the hexagon

Pakistan is the only country in the region whose internal politics and state fault lines are casting a shadow of instability, not only in South and Central Asia but around the globe too. Pakistan, thus, is badly affecting the neighborhood through its hexagonal state chemistry and characteristic. The 'Punjabization' of the state apparatus; cultural 'Urduization'; non-indigenous takeover of the deep-state (by the 1947 refugees of Punjabi, Urdu and Kashmiri origin); dominancy of the ethno-linguistic Punjabi minority on the rest; imposition of the sectarian Wahabi-Salafi Muslim minority over the rest of the Muslims, Hindus and Christians; and finally, the militarization of almost all state and non-state apparatus is the hexagonal statehood that is causing instability in Southasia and state failure in Pakistan.

Averting state-failure as well as ensuring peace, stability and security in Southasia depends on dismantling these hexagonal bonds in the state molecules of Pakistan. This ultimately means drastic reforms and paradigm shift in the state, society, and politics of Pakistan.

The primary task for avoiding the possible break-up of Pakistan and ensuring stability, peace, and Southasian regionalization is to fulfill the fundamental task of electing a Constituent Assembly (CA) for the first time in the history of Pakistan. The CA should have a mandate to legislate and regularize ethnic balance in the armed forces and security agencies based on the proportionate participation of Sindhi, Punjabi, Baloch, Pashtun, Siraki, Hindko, Balti and Urdu speaking Sindhis; guarantee the indigenous majority's demographic sovereignty in their historical provinces; the separation of religion from the state; banning violent Madaris; change in the nomenclature as well as legislative authority of the 'Provincial Assemblies' into 'Legislative State Assemblies'; and abolishing the bar on Hindus, Christians and Ahmadiyas for holding the offices of the President, Prime Minister, chiefs of the armed forces and security agencies. Restricting the role of military to border defense and change in state-ideology from a two nation theory into Indus nationhood would be a step forward. Pakistan being renamed a Union of Indus States would certainly change the course of Southasian polity and equity. If the institution of the President is continued, the governors of the provinces/states should be elected through the Provincial Legislative Assemblies, whilst the institution of the Presidency should be made ceremonious.

If these very basic reforms are not made, the emergence of Sindh and Balochistan as sovereign countries can become inevitable. Prime Minister Sharif, if willing, can perform this noble job during his term or even after completing his five years tenure.

Neighborly learning

Pakistan in fact needs to adopt the better federal practices of other neighbor countries, for example India, which on the demand of Tamil Nadu state, recently sent a Foreign Minister to the Commonwealth meeting of state-heads in Sri Lanka. Likewise, a refugee's adoption here also needs the consent of the state (provincial) government where the refugee intends to settle. Besides, a Prime Minister in India resolves major issues through joint online conference with the Chief Ministers and the cabinet. Moreover, barrage land, which is precious in the arid desert of Rajasthan, cannot normally be purchased by the first generation of internal migrants from other Indian states. Similarly, a non-Kashmiri usually cannot be a caretaker of a Hindu temple in Kashmir. None can be a minister in another state, unlike Pakistan where Punjabis and Pashtuns usually become ministers in Sindh; however, such a practice has never been seen in Punjab, Balochistan and Khyber Pakhtunkhuwa provinces.

Road to one Southasia

The demographic composition of Sindh and to certain extent Balochistan is being altered at the behest of the Pakistani establishment, which has adopted British tactics of occupying colonies by shifting its own or friendly populations over to other lands. Punjabi, Afghani Pashtun, Rohangyan Muslim and other Muslim origin refugees from across the world are mostly being settled in Sindh and Balochistan, thus creating demographic insecurities for locals. Besides, a US and Turkish assessment has unveiled that Sindh houses the largest reserves of gas, oil and coal in Southasia. Therefore, Punjab and Urdu speakers are trying to take hold of the province. Amid such a contest over land and natural resources, demographic insecurities and indigenous people's right to rule their historical motherlands, the people of Sindh and Balochistan will never welcome a borderless Southasia and a visa-free India-Pakistan until the federal structure and state chemistry is altered.

Recent developments and the thawing of US-Iran relations will further reduce the strategic importance of Pakistan in Asia, thereby creating an avenue to nullify the clientalism, corporatism and monopoly of the military and its dominating ethnic Punjabis over the rest of Pakistan. Visa-free India-Pakistan is impossible without state as well as federal reforms in Pakistan. One Southasia is not possible without reforms in Pakistan.

Published in daily The Kathmandu Post, Nepal on December 22, 2013

Unmasking Democracy: Military versus Civil Governance in Sindh

After a month of the millions' march in Karachi for the freedom of Sindh, the Sindh Assembly for the first time in its history within Pakistan has unanimously passed a resolution on April 29, 2014 against the Federal Government and the Federation of Pakistan. The resolution mentioning "accesses done by the Federal Governments of Pakistan against Sindh" and has quoted that the Federation of Pakistan is punishing Sindh [...].

It is worth mentioning here that Sindh Assembly was once called 'Sindh Legislative Assembly' of the 'State of Sindh' before the creation of Pakistan in 1947. The head of Sindh Government was then called Prime Minister. Besides, the independent and sovereign governments of Britannia (United Kingdom) and Sindh held more than a dozen treaties for trade, military and technical exchange between two the sovereign countries before 1843. Contrary to this, if seen today, astonishing is the fact that current head of Sindh Government called Chief Minister (ruling Sindh since last ten years) hitherto has been dubbed as the weaker most head of the federating province in Pakistan has for the first time started talking unexpectedly.

In fact, Sindhi intelligentsia has remained worried over the reality that Sindh, which was historically having surplus budget until 1965 has gradually underwent fiscal decline inversely proportionate to its major and rising share in the economy, revenues, and natural resources abundance of Pakistan. It is common among the Sindhi literati that the 'authority' and 'autonomy' of Sindh Government has shirked anti-clockwise after the partition of 1947, and the powers of Chief Minister of Sindh have skewed as much as of the 'Political Agents' of Pakistan establishment installed in the

Federally Administered Tribal Areas (FATA). A 'Political Agent' in Pakistan is acting only on the orders of the Federal Government of Pakistan.

The hitherto untold account of the state-within-state or the third state in terms of governance in Sindh stretches from town level local government (Panchayat) to the provincial level Sindh Government. The military establishment of Pakistan comprising the dominated Punjabis is the real decision approver of these two tiers of governance in Sindh, which is part of federation of Pakistan since last seven decades. This state-within-state or Third State situation has been the real fault lines of the friction and conflicts between Sindh and Federation as well as mother of all illnesses in Sindh.

Town and Tehsil Mayors versus Captains and Majors

Usually a Town / Panchayat elected leader of the local government tiers needs a semi-clearance from the all non-civil and civil-intelligence agencies of not only the criminal record but also of the ideological record based on the ideological bent. If someone is communist; an outspoken secular; unbeliever of two-nation theory; Sindhi nationalist, there are no chances for his clearance. He has to bid a compromise, and start practicing Namaz at least once a month, praise two nations' theory and condemn Hindus role in the united India; disown his or her ideology. Otherwise, he or she should be ready to face election troubles trouble, especially election frauds. Mostly officials ranking from Captain to Majors of Pakistan Army are virtual command in enormous matters of the local governance at Town and Tehsil level.

Simultaneously, a District Nazim / City Government Mayor is required to get clearance on the above lines, have to take instructions by the Pakistan Army's sitting Colonel / Lt. Colonel deputed in the district for the intelligence coordination among the civil and non civil intelligence outfits. This position of Colonel behaves as a virtual Governor of the district. No District or City Nazim / Mayor can take major decisions without getting final approval from the military official.

Major-Brigadiers versus Colleges and Universities

A higher education collage in towns and cities of the province are virtually dealt as Collage Districts. The principals of these districts ought to keep close coordination and liaison with the *Tehsil* military official mostly of Captains or sometimes a senior holding the post of Major or Lt. Colonel. Simultaneously no university in Sindh is autonomous to take their academic, administrative, and extra-curricular activities. A Brigadier of Pakistan Army is the final virtual authority. A Vice Chancellor of a university cannot take major decision in the above domains without his nod.

Sindh Assembly versus Corpse V Karachi

Almost all proceedings of Sindh Assembly are real-time observed by the intelligence section working under the Corpse Commander of Corpse V of the Pakistan Army in Karachi, who is officially in-charge for the military actions and operations in Sindh and Balochistan provinces. A hopeful / aspirant of the Member Province Assembly (MPA) must possess an intelligence clearance by the Military Intelligence, ISI and IB in Sindh and he or she should be a firm believer of Two Nations Theory or Muslim Nationhood in Pakistan and must not be a Sindhi nationalist and preferably should not have visited India before becoming the MPA. If someone qualifies on the above lines, there are some chances for the candidates that their elections results would not be rigged.

Corps Commander Sindh versus Chief Minister Sindh

Crops Commanders of Pakistan Army in Sindh were once termed "Karor (millions) Commanders" by the slain Prime Minister Benazir Bhutto. It is a well known fact among the journalist and political circles of Sindh that every newly appointed Corps Commander of Karachi joins dinner discussion with the outgoing one, and the outgoing one put a challenge to the new official for more kickbacks from Sindh than what he earned in his duration as a Corps Commander.

The Chief Minister's secretariat and the major decisions by the Chief Minister Sindh regarding the province need to be agreed un-constitutionally by the Corps Commander Karachi.

Militarized Corruption

Reducing the security expenditures, the military in Sindh takes Public Service Commission (PCS) and Civil Service Commission (CSS) officers into their intelligence fold. They are not paid for their loyalty and un-constitutional services to the Military Intelligence and ISI; however they are assured for unchecked corruption in lieu of their 'services' and loyalty for the military.

Given these circumstance, there are less possibilities for Sindh Assembly, Sindh Government, and Local Government to take bold policy, political and administrative decisions protecting interests of the people of Sindh particularly Sindhis. The situation is a naïve example of 'State-within-State' or 'Third State' versus 'Sindh Government'. This is the drawback behind the underdevelopment, law and order situation, growing religious extremism and educational institutions failure in Sindh.

Can Sindh or rest of Pakistan undergo the reforms in this direction? The chances are thin and non-existent. Would Sindh finally decide to secede from Pakistan to protect the future of more than 50 million people? Answer lies in the Bhawisher Wani (The Book of Future).

Published on www.merinews.com on May 01, 2014

An Open Letter to Hasina Wajid

We owe you applause, your Excellency Sheikh Hasina Wajid, for your government's significant steps in bringing the perpetrators of war crimes in 1971 to justice. This expression of cheer by a Sindhi in exile is the continuity of an earlier generation of Sindhis and Balochs who shed blood tears over heart-wrecking brutalities, like massacres and rapes, rendered by the Pakistan Army in 1971 in Bangladesh. The political, social, and literary leadership of that time in Sindh and Balochistan in Pakistan was supporting Banglabandhu Sheikh Mujibur Rehman. Hundreds, if not thousands, took to the streets of Sindh cities and towns against the military operation in Bangladesh (then East Pakistan). Although, Sindhis and Balochs themselves are today facing gradual an ethnic cleansing-like situation.

War crimes

Humanity can never forgive those who killed three million civilians and raped hundreds of thousands of innocent women with the support of the military-supported right-wing terrorists of Al-Shams and Al-Badar in Bangladesh, who were outfits of Jamait-e-Islami Pakistan. Unfortunately, these local butchers were ethno-linguistically non-Bengalis of Bihari origin, who were playing the same tune as a Karachi-based party of refugees (muhajirs) has been playing in Sindh for the last two decades at the behest of Pakistan's security establishment.

It was the political course of 1960s. The Awami League of Sheikh Mujibur Rehman had a relatively strong existence in Sindh after East Pakistan. Both Sindh and East Bengal together fought against the banning of Sindhi and Bengali languages and the introduction of a One-Unit federal mechanism by the military regimes of General Ayub and Yahya Khan. The vote bank of Sindh was divided along the lines of the supporters of Benazir Bhutto and the supporters of Sheikh Mujibur Rehman. Political icons like G M Sayyed, Qazi Faiz Mohammad and many others were staunch critics of the ethnic Punjabi domination of Pakistan and thus, lost their seats due to rigging engineered by the military regime of General Yahya Khan.

In commemoration

In early 1972, a highly popular Sindhi nationalist-cum-leftist leader Rasool Bux Palijo wrote the first ever book on Bangladesh war crimes and organized a peasant protest in Sindh for the freedom of Sheikh Mujibur Rehman while also demanding action against military officials accused of war crimes. As expected in a militarized country like Pakistan, the Hammod Rehman (Judicial) Commission was constituted to inquire into the war crimes and secession of Bangladesh. However, the commission's crucial findings and observations have not yet been made public and nor has the guilty military leadership been punished.

It is also worth appreciating that your government has bestowed awards to the G M Sayyed, Qazi Faiz Ahmed and Anwar Pirzado from Sindh and Ghous Bux Bizanjo from Balochistan for their support of the Bengali people during the 1971 military operation. Although your second lieutenants forgot to include Rasool Bux Palijo in the list, a Lahore-based Punjabi activist-cum-lawyer, who like other Punjabis, kept mum over the war crimes during 1971, has also been given an award.

Similarly, the Punjab-born prominent Urdu progressive poet Faiz Ahmed Faiz was also given an award for his poem 'Hum ke thahrey ajnabi, itni mulaqaton ke baad'. Faiz chose 'Suqot-e-Dhaka' (The Fall of Dhaka) as the title for a poem. But the poem is in fact an expression of grief over the separation of East Pakistan from the West, not a condemnation of war crimes against Bengalis during the eight-month military campaign. Activists, journalists and intellectuals of that era in Pakistan recall when Faiz, who was a retired captain of the army, was interviewed by BBC Radio Urdu Service during the military operation in Bengal. He announced that he would return the Lenin Peace Prize if the Soviet Union did not stop supporting the Bengali secessionists.

To the ICC

Bengal won its freedom from the ethnic monopoly of Punjab. The rest of the people in Pakistan are still undergoing a form of apartheid. Since your government has already started cleaning house, the time has come to take one-step forward. Criminals in the Pakistan military and their cronies in the Pakistani establishment need to be taken to the International Criminal Court (ICC) for their war crimes in Bangladesh. Such an initiative will be true justice for the thousands of civilians killed and raped. This will not only inch Bangladesh towards international justice but also prove to be great support to the oppressed peoples of Sindh, Balochistan and Pakhtunkhuwa in Pakistan, as well as a long-term bailout for peace and security in Southasia.

There is no iota of possibility for the sustenance of internal social movement to demilitarize Pakistan's polity and society and offer salvation to the people of Sindh and Balochistan from the ethnic hegemony of Punjab. Bangladesh going to the ICC would permanently restrict the Pakistani military from derailing democracy and prevent them from committing crimes against humanity concerning Sindhi, Baloch, Hindu, Christians and Ahmadi people. Moreover, the military would then limit itself to defense affairs and avoid interfering in the political arena of the country. Such a step would be a great contribution to the stability and security of Southasia. Joy Bangla! Joy Sindh! Long live the Indus people!

Published in daily The Kathmandu Post on January 13, 2014

Social Movements: Where Does Sindh Stand In The World?

'Peacefulness' was a diplomatic phrase, if not a jargon, of the twentieth century – a time when 'world' was not transformed into a conscious and highly connected 'globe'. The bent of international and regional actors towards engaging with the peaceful and violent movements can simplistically but truly termed as political and strategic hypocrisy. How the world today positions itself towards peaceful social and political movements? A ten-million dollar question, indeed!

One can react while reading this unfashionable term of 'political and strategic hypocrisy'; however, it is very simple of understand. An interest based tagging for the legitimacy of violent and illegitimacy of peaceful movements. If seen in the perspective of international community's approach towards different political and social movements, the wishful tagging of the terms like 'peaceful', 'non-violent' or the 'violent' becomes a phenomenal disposition of the interest based approach. One can conclude that there is a conflict of approaches in the world – interest based versus justice based. In many a cases, interest based approach has been adopted repeatedly by the various states and powers. Meanwhile, justice based approach is paradoxically owned by the peoples. Numerous movements in the various continents have been encountering this phenomenal dilemma.

There are at least three significant sets of the major social and political movements in the world – slow-paced movements around socio-economic justice; the Arab-spring style movement for the democratic governance; and the movements for the territorial liberation.

Most of the movements based on socio-economic justice have an outlook of the structural and legal reforms for the socio-economic justice for the women, transgender and marginalized sections of the societies; hence they are not only peaceful but also are supported by the governments as well as international forums. No government bothers thinking their tagging in terms of peaceful or violent. They mostly are catered through the international development funds, which are pipelined via international development aid programs of various developed countries as well as international and regional financial interest groups and bodies of various socio-political outfits.

The Arab Spring style movements have been both peaceful and violent simultaneously; and the majority among the international community has never shown their concern about their being peaceful or violence. This is what we can say strategic hypocrisy where the principle of peacefulness is sidelined over the niche of interests.

The victim most of the socio-political movements are of the territorial liberation in the various parts of the world, which have always gathered this typical fuss of jargonized terms of 'violent' versus 'peaceful'. No doubt, most of the freedom movements around the world are violent; however, the hypocrisy of the world community becomes extraordinarily visible when they start measuring and considering the issues. They, hitherto, only have prioritized the violent movements over the peaceful ones. The case of Palestine, Kosovo, Kurdistan, and Tamil Elam has always attracted focus of not only the various countries but also of the regional forums like European Union and Arab League as well as various bodies of the United Nations. Kashmir does not fall in this category, although there is an oldest UN resolution regarding it. Kashmir can be set out of the matrix because the violence acknowledge and attributed with Kashmir has been based on non-Kashmiri Jihadists from the Punjab province of Pakistan. Contrary to this, there is at least one highly populist and massive movement for the freedom and self-determination of Sindh in Pakistan, which is very little known to the world outside despite the fact that the movement dates back to the movement for the liberation of Bangladesh.

There is a highly power high scale insurgency and war in Balochistan, and no doubt, it has been successful to attain international attention. Since Baloch are around six million in the hilly and mountainous province forming sixty percent area of Pakistan, therefore they are unable to make a pressurizing public outpour; hence expecting a peaceful movement in Balochistan is out of question.

If one reviews Sindhi newspapers of the last sixty-nine years, one surprises to see that this homeland of 50 million Sindhis have never been silent. Activism and movement building in the form of hunger strikes, protest sit-ins, inter and intra cities on-foot marches, rallies, shutter down strikes and vehicular jam strikes has always occupied the newspapers. However, Sindhi uprising during last five years has not only been exceptional but phenomenal as well.

In 2008, a Sindhi nationalist party Jeay Sindh Qomi Mahaz (JSQM) held Sindh Freedom March in almost every district of Sindh, which was attended by thousands of the people. On November 7, 2009, on the party's call for Sindh Freedom March, at least 2.5 hundred thousand people gathered in the city and demanded the world powers and the United Nations an independent and sovereign status, in which British invaded it in 1843. Invasion of Sindh in 1843 was a violation of various treaties between the Emirs of Sindh and Royal deputies of the Great Britain.

On March 23, 2012, JSQM again held a Sindh Freedom March attended by two million Sindhis. Talking to the 'Freedom March' JSQM leader Bashir Qureshi announced Sindh bidding farewell the historical Resolution of Pakistan that was adopted on March 23, 1940. He also sought international community's help in this regard. He was killed through poison on April 8, 2012.

On March 23, 2014, JSQM again organized 'Sindh Freedom March' in Karachi. At least five million people according to the various international and Sindh based print and electronic media houses. To pressurize JSQM for cancelation of the Freedom March, the top leader of the JSQM and brother of Bashir Qureshi, Maqsood Qureshi was gunned down and later on burnt down to the ashes by the "security agencies of Pakistan." According to the JSQM leadership, they were already under pressure by the state agencies asking them to cancel the Freedom March. While addressing the mammoth gathering, JSQM Chairperson Sunan Qureshi demanded United Nations, the USA, UK, France, Russia, and China for their intervention and support for the independence of Sindh. Unlike some portions of Western, Middle East and Afghan media, the news found no space in South Asian media.

The overall trend and the tilt of ignorance and negligence by the media, governments and to certain extent international forums toward this peaceful movement of South Asia would one day possibly push them to become violent. A neglected and underestimated highly popular peaceful movement usually turns into the violent one.

It is quit convincing that under-estimating a peaceful popular movement would mean that world has no space for the peaceful movements, hence a highly peaceful movement may possibly turn into the violent one.

Despite apparently professing peace and non-violence agenda around the globe, the political and strategic hypocrisy by the world powers regarding movement of Sindh will add up into chaos in the South Asia. This is the prime opportunity, when the world by focusing a peaceful movement can set an example that international community prefers peaceful socio-political movements to the radical and violent one.

Let the world set at least first example to prioritize this peaceful movement before it is too late. The time has come, when the world community needs to avoid political and strategic hypocrisy and set example for the world politics of dissenting social movements.

Published in Daily Afghanistan Times, April 13, 2014

The New Neutral

When individual or collective conflicts push politics into a blind alley, neutrality becomes key to mediation and resolution. Mediation, in all its forms—cultural, individual, collective or judicial—requires neutrality. If seen through the lens of diplomatic history among nations and the cultural history of people, neutrality embodied with justice has not only been successful in bringing about peace but also sustaining it. Hence, the diversified nature of conflicts, inter- as well as intra-state, ethnic and group require the exhibition of extreme neutrality for a judicious and sustainable resolution of the antagonism that is destined to lead all of us towards collective destruction.

No sides to take

Inter- and intra-state, ethnic and national conflicts have frequently occurred in the post-modern world. The post-World War League of Nations, which culminated into the UN, was an outcome of many international/European treaties among nations, which were neither judicious nor brokered by neutral mediators. Hence, it provided a reason for World War II. The two World Wars were waged between colonizers and aspirants holding colonial ambitions, seeking maximum control over colonies and their wealth and natural resources. Thus, the birth of the UN became inevitable since a neutral body was the niche of the modern era of statehood. Meanwhile, the powerful among the countries also formed parallel alliances at regional and international levels to further their interests.

No doubt, the UN has gradually transcended into a comparatively neutral forum since the world needed to go a step forward to formulate an international legal framework, not only for the member states but also for the citizens of member states. However, it is the our duty to introduce further reforms, agree upon new legal and policy frameworks, reform the structure and the authority to exhibit maximum neutrality and impartiality.

Nations, governments and international institutions always have to deal with a complex patchwork of relations and behaviors when they have to switch between neutrality and securing their interests. Since national interest has mostly superseded justice and neutrality in interest-based competitions, diplomacy and internal-external engagements, neutrality today has become an absurdity. This was evident in the recent political crises in Syria and Ukraine. It has also been observed in the Israel-Palestine conflict, the Kurdistan Movement, the Tibetan issue and the freedom movement in Sindh and Balochistan in Pakistan.

In fact, the absence of justice-based neutrality, both in nation-states and international and regional forums like the UN, Saarc and the Organization of Islamic Countries, despite coming up with remedies have also been deepening the old wounds of the people. This has resulted in the rise of gross human rights violations, ethnic cleansing and war crimes that victimize millions of innocent citizens and dissenters.

Power biases

Power and interest-based politics and diplomacy have also given birth to another kind of discrimination. It is based on a discriminatory approach towards social leadership from the perspective of the oppressed or less powerful nations and ethnicities vis-à-vis monopolists and the powerful. The phenomenon is exclusively seen in broader civil society, which includes activists, journalists, writers, analysts, intellectuals, lawyers and other professionals. Usually, social leadership, associated with powerful ethnic groups, command more centrality and acceptability than leaders from among the group of oppressed people.

The phenomenon is more visible in the developing world, particularly in South Asian societies where social, institutional and structural development has historically been built around power.

Pakistan, Bangladesh and Nepal are the best examples of this tilt. Since the Pakistani state and power corridors, for example, are monopolized by ethnic Punjabi allied with the Urdu-speaking elite, the rest of the South Asian and the world societies have an unintentional bias towards the social leadership of Sindhi, Balochi, Pashtun and Siraki origin vis-à-vis those of Punjabi and Urdu origin. This further intensifies issues of high importance and complex nature. The leadership of Punjabi and Urdu origin in Pakistan is well connected with the state, to which they have historically been given agency to participate in decision making. Their input is usually sought after by the establishment in almost all significant internal and external decision making. Besides, they also defend, in numerous cases, even unjustifiable decisions by the state in international forums in an overt or covert manner.

On the other hand, the leadership from Sindh, Balochistan, Khyber Pakhtunkhuwa and Siraiki Southern Punjab has been contributing intellectually to the social and political movements for rights. The journalists, human rights activists, scholars, intellectuals, academicians and literati from these provinces are not only discriminated within Pakistan but also during professional and thematic forums held regionally and internationally.

Similarly, when Baloch or Sindhi journalists, activists and thinkers are persecuted or killed by the state forces, the regional and international media and civil society seldom give them attention. However, when people of Punjabi and Urdu origin from the same professions—which are usually attached to certain layers of the establishment—are victimized, it becomes a matter of concern in regional and international forums.

If the Sindhi or Baloch leadership sympathizes with the political movement of their people and victims of persecution, the world outside criminalizes them. None would even think for the moment that the civil society and media associates and advisors of dominant ethnic groups in Pakistan have also an intellectual share in the crimes against humanity committed by the state. They are generally treated as credible entities. This inability to differentiate between social and civil leadership of the oppressed and the oppressor even by the leadership of other countries is also a kind of bias. Their unwillingness to see perceive both the parties as equals is also a kind of discrimination. It is an exhibition of the people-to-people or civil non-neutrality. This attitude is not only found among individuals but also those in highly reputable rights bodies, media houses, think tanks and intellectuals.

New ethos

A similar problem persists on a lower scale and in different forms when the leadership from the smaller countries, mostly with a single majority ethnic-construct like Nepal, Bangladesh, the Maldives and Bhutan engage and interact with their counterparts from the rest of the developing world. The non-existence of a neutral human interaction and people-to-people contact are more dangerous than that the foreign policies of the establishments of developing countries.

The critical mass of human rights, civil, political and economic justice and peace has grown in the last two decades. This larger tribe of activists, experts, journalists, writers, intellectuals, academicians and other professionals usually identifies itself with the various aspects and levels of social justice. Paradoxically, it lacks justice within its own tribe when it comes to supporting and sympathizing with victims or being neutral when it's a case of the oppressed versus the dominant. This not only applies to broader civil society but also international bodies. A new ethos needs to replace old biases, discrimination and non-neutrality, primarily in people's diplomacy.

Published in Daily The Kathmandu Post, Nepal

Sindhi Nationalism through the Kaleidoscope of History

The history of Sindhi nationalism is basically a history of resistance movements and wars fought against foreign invasions across the centuries. Modern Sindhi nationalism, however, begins with the resistance against the British in the mid-nineteenth century. The entire movement can be divided into two parts: pre- and post-Partition.

1842 – 1900: The Talpurs' war and the Hur Guerrilla Movement

The pre-Partition wave begins with the Talpurs' war in 1842. This period, due to its characteristics, can be referred to as the 'early resistance' period (1842-1900), in which Sindh was conquered by Charles Napier at Miani near Hyderabad in March 1943 and annexed with the Bombay presidency. Insurgencies, however, immediately dominated the scene, beginning with uprising of Ranas under Karan Singh on April 15, 1859, in Tharparkar, a south-eastern desert district. Hundreds of fighters lost their lives in this insurgency, which was followed by mutiny in the army in Mirpurkhas and Karachi.

A severe blow to the British rule in Sindh, however, was given by first Hur Guerrilla Movement in 1890 under the leadership of Syed Mardan Shah, the grandfather of Pakistan Muslim League-Functional (PML-F) chief Pir Pagaro. Hundreds of fighters took part in this war, which continued for no less than a decade. Three main participants of this phase of the movement, however, caught the public eye. They were Bachu Badshah, Peeru Vazir and Gulu Government.

1900 – 1940: Socio-economic transformations and the rise of feudalism

The British, after conquering Sindh, patronized feudalism by offering an enormous number of fertile agriculture lands to individuals who pledged loyalty to the new Colonial rulers. A new phase of socio-economic development began, which can be identified as a transitional period (1900-1940).

Three quarters of the population comprised Muslims, while the remaining was Hindu. The majority of Hindus, traditionally, were shopkeepers, traders and professionals living in the urban hubs, while the Muslims remained landowners, tillers and herdsmen living in small villages, hamlets and remote huts. At the time of the British conquest only one million acres of land were irrigated. The population of Sindh was about 1.4 million, with about 25 per cent Hindus.

The British transformed Sindh from medieval to modern through changes in the infrastructure, communication, education and the system of governance. Sindh was separated from Bombay and the Sindh Legislative Assembly was established in Karachi later in the 1930s. During this, Sindh supported the formation process of the Indian National Army under Subhash Chandra Bose and some young Sindhis also carried out some militant activities, which included blasts at several railway tracks. They were also involved in well-known bomb blasts in Delhi at the time.

1941 – 1943: The Hurs re-emerge

The second Hur Guerrilla Warfare period began in early 1941, under Sibghatullah Shah, the father of PML-F chief, Pir Pagaro. An area of about 25,000 square kilometers was converted into a battleground between the guerrillas and the British forces. To counter this, some 35,000 troops from the Baloch and Punjab regiments were installed in Sindh. Heavy artillery was also used, and eventually the first Martial Law in the history of the subcontinent was imposed in Sindh.

Post-Partition: Exodus of the middle class and the emergence of 'cultural nationalism'

Sindh fought for its liberation for a hundred years, from 1843 to 1943. The partition of United India and the creation of Pakistan, however, was partially the result of the G.M Syed-led polity in Sindh from 1943 to 1947. Syed later disowned this.

The creation of Pakistan, in its very beginning proved to be initiation of a new devastation in the social and national tranquility of Sindh. An exodus of Sindhi Hindus from the province created a vacuum in society because they formed the sole petty-bourgeois and bourgeois classes of Sindh. The space left by them was occupied by immigrants from India who had a different culture and language and could not merge with Sindhi society as perfectly as was aspired by the leadership of the Muslim League Sindh. Besides, Karachi was separated from Sindh and was given to the federal government as the capital of the country.

In 1954, the One Unit scheme was introduced to counter the numerical majority of East Pakistan. This laid the foundation of the destruction of Sindhi culture and gave Punjab the authority over the natural resources of the province. Between 1947 and 1970, Sindhi nationalism, sans the middle class, adopted the form of cultural nationalism.

1970 - 1990s: Z.A Bhutto, MRD, and nationalist resistance to military rule

It was Z.A Bhutto, the founder and first chairman of the Pakistan People's Party (PPP), who began transformation of Sindhi society by developing its middle class, this laying the foundations for social transition in Sindh. This undoubtedly influenced the Sindhi nationalist movement in form as well as content. After Bhutto's execution, Sindh entered a decade-long resistance against the military; causing hundreds of civil and military causalities. In its essence, the Movement for the Restoration of Democracy (MRD) in Sindh was a nationalist resistance rather than a movement for democracy.

Soon after General Ziaul Haq's death, the PPP came into power again, opening the corridors of opportunities for the people of Sindh, including the recently-born middle class, political cadres, and others. Thus, nationalist tendencies in Sindhi society become relatively milder than earlier. Contrary to this, the picture changed entirely during the regime of General (retd) Pervez Musharraf.

December 27, 2007: The tide turns

After the murder of PPP Chairperson (and daughter of PPP founder Z.A Bhutto) Benazir Bhutto, nationalist tendencies in Sindh achieved mass outlook. A manifestation of this was witnessed during the first three days of her murder (she was assassinated in Rawalpindi on December 27, 2007).

As soon as the current PPP government completes its tenure, the new boom in Sindhi nationalism will become more visible. In the future course, it may take the Urdu-speaking community as a major ally. In fact, a new definition of contemporary Sindhi nationalism by cobbling together two linguistic parts -- Sindhi and Urdu -- can provide the foundation of a new form of Sindhi nationalism.

Published in daily The News, Karachi on June 19, 2009

STATE VERSUS PEOPLE

A Tale of Strategic Talbanization

The recent military campaign 'Zarb-e-Azb' by Pakistan Army in Afghanistan bordering tribal areas against Taliban, Al-Qaida and their Pakistani, Central Asian and Arab fugitive recruits continues to occupy news and analysis. Like previous ones, this recent military campaign was of no significant result, thus compelling the United States to drone strategically important "Punjabi Talban Headquarters" on July 19. Due to the changing complexion of religiosity and terrorism in Pakistan, a review of the military move is needed in the perspective of Talbanization in Southern Pakistan.

A fruitless move

There are some commonalities in the recent and the previous military campaigns launched in the Pashtun tribal areas. The campaign, like previous ones, has been selective, in which certain terrorists were targeted, meanwhile the rest were given space to flee into adjacent tribal, semi-tribal and provincial areas of Southern Khyber Pakhtunkhuwa, Sindh and Balochistan provinces. A larger part of the terrorists were Punjabi Taliban, hence was deliberately excluded from the campaign through political tactics of negotiations. The campaign also caused a massive human displacement and, like in the past, it was used as a safe passage for establishment's 'blue eyed boys'.

The army avoided or failed to touch the hardcore infrastructure of terrorist coordination in the tribal areas, of which a large number of secular citizens from Southern Pakistan believe is run by Punjabi Taliban. They are considered to be the recruiters and strategists behind the tribal Pashtun Taliban. They were droned by the United States, which were called a concrete achievement by the vernacular media reports in the decade-long history of droning at Af-Pak borders. In fact, the Punjabi Talban is the real culprit of the terrorism in Central and South Asia, and is deceptively protected by the security establishment.

Strategic deception

Why is the menace of Talbanization and religious extremism, despite many efforts, dominating Pakistani scene? The answer is simple: the military establishment is playing a microcosmic game of strategic deception aimed at creating a strategic swamp on the both side of river Indus. It's a bid to create another virtual Shat-al-Arab, or a highly modulated Warfield in Pakistan on the lines of Iraq, a kind of strategic swamp against NATO, India, Afghanistan and the Central Asian States, probably with the support of Petro-Riyals.

Many know in Pakistan, however reluctant they are to speak out, that Pakistan's military establishment itself creates Taliban and religious extremists, uses them and finally separates the experts and the most loyal "terrorist assets," and gives them safe passage whenever the world outside pressures Pakistan to launch a military offense. This microcosmic game is generally expressed by the political circles of Southern Pakistan, especially Sindhi and Baloch as "creating ten Taliban, killing five upon international pressure to acquire external military support".

Sindhi and Baloch nationalists believe that Talbanization of Southern Pakistan and military offensive in northern Pakistan are strategically connected for transporting Salafi terrorists en masse to the natural resource-rich and culturally diverse Sufi Sindh and Balochistan. It is a common view among Sindhi and Baloch that the military as well as espionage technology that is acquired by Pakistan from the West, particularly from the US, is mostly used against Sindhi and Balch nationalists, secessionists, uncompromising journalists and the vocal civil rights activists.

The indigenous people of Southern Pakistan believe "Quetta Shura" is the strategic deception for the "Rawalpindi Shura." The Pakistani army wants to use this deceptive propaganda to protect extremist hardcore leadership and launch offense against the Baloch movement. The July 15 *New York Times* story by Saba Imtiaz and Declan Walsh mentioning thousands of extremist seminaries in Southern Pakistan is also indicative of that microcosmic game. It can be assumed that Pakistan is now gradually shifting its anti-

India infiltrative terror machinery from Pakistan-held Kashmir and Punjab to India bordering Sindh.

Demography and Talbanization

Federalism in Pakistan is the monopoly of Punjabi and the Urdu-speaking Muhajir elite over the rest. This ethnic monopoly has the peculiar trait of changing demographic complexion, particularly through settlements of Punjabi and their allied ethnic groups in Sindh, Balochistan and Siraiki South Punjab. The sixty-seven years of demographic internal-colonialism in Pakistan has alarmed Sindh, Balochistan and Siraiki South Punjab, where the indigenous and local population is gradually being turned into minority. It has also been used for countering anti-military dictatorship and secessionist movements. Sindhi and Baloch, traditionally Sufi and secular, understand that the injection of Salafi extremism into their lands are the proxy infrastructure similar to Salafi Al-Shams and Al-Badr outfits in Bangladesh that may be used for controlling their natural resources and countering secessionist movements.

Transformative engagement

Transformation of Pakistan from a militaristic state, and northern Pakistan especially Punjab from epicenter and importer of Salafi terrorism into a moderate society, is the biggest challenge for international security. Eliminating the roots of religious extremism and terrorism from Pakistan essentially requires a cleansing of Punjabi-dominated military and security establishment in Pakistan, which would be impossible without engaging and strengthening the utmost secular Sindhi, Baloch, Pashtun and Siraiki nationalists.

Published on Truthout, USA on July 26, 2014

Pakistan: What Does The Future Hold?

Pakistan is at a crossroads. Its fragmented internal and external political situation is gradually inching towards chaos. The key to understanding these current crises is in the understanding of state building and statecraft.

The country is facing secessionist movements in the Balochistan and Sindh provinces; religious terrorism in Punjab, the Tribal Areas, and Khyber Pakhtunkhwa (KPK) province; war on its Afghan border; continued discontent with neighboring India; disagreements with the US; and a distancing from Saudi Arabia.

Ethnography of state building

Pakistan's foreign policy is deeply rooted in the partition of British India, and thereby in the early period of its state building.

In 1946, Pashtuns, under Khan Abdul Ghaffar Khan, were against the idea of Pakistan. They were considered an internal security threat by the Muhajir (refugees from India) leadership of the All India Muslim League (AIML), and as a result the NWFP (now KPK) Provincial Legislative Assembly which housed a congressional majority was dismissed in September 1947.

Sindh was treated similarly. G.M. Syed, who tabled and lobbied the historic Resolution of Pakistan in the Sindh Legislative Assembly before the partition, became an arch opponent of it in 1946 and resigned from the AIML. The Sindh government was dismissed in

April 1948 due to their refusal to separate Karachi from Sindh in order to establish a capital of the newly formed country and its resistance of violence against the Hindu population of the area and their exodus.

Balochistan was neither part of the partition plan nor was it part of Pakistan in 1947. Qalat Khanate (Balochi speaking Balochistan) was an independent sovereign state with a bicameral parliament, cabinet and a head of the state. Balochistan was annexed to Pakistan in 1948.

Sindhis, Balochis and Pashtuns were perceived to be a security concern by the Punjabi-Muhajir AIML leadership, military and civil bureaucracy, and were excluded from the state building process. The foreign policy making of Pakistan, excluding Zulfiqar Ali Bhutto's period of 1972-1977, was been envisioned, steered, and implemented by the ethnic-Punjabi majority army in association with Urdu Speaking the Muhajir majority bureaucracy. If analyzed on the ethnic lines, the Ministry of Foreign Affairs in Pakistan have employed fewer ethnic Sindhis and Balochs in last sixty years then the ethnic Punjabis and Urdu speaking Muhajirs employed during last sixty months.

In 1947, the army was almost entirely Punjabi, whilst the civil bureaucracy and the AIML leadership was Muhajir. The AIML leadership being refugees did not have an electoral constituency in Pakistan, and there democracy was less aligned with their interests. Moreover, Jinnah's practical detachment from state-building due to his deteriorated health led Pakistan towards a non-democratic political model based on a civil bureaucracy-military-aristocracy triumvirate of Punjabi and Urdu speaking refugees, which kept the other ethnicities and provinces away from the processes of state craft. Pakistan's foreign policy towards India could be defined as a reaction of the Punjabi and Urdu-speaking refugees towards the violence occurred during the partition.

Since the formation of Pakistan, Pashtuns were sidelined to prevent their imagined annexation with Afghanistan. The NWFP region was accorded to British India under Durand Line agreement in 1893 by Afghan King Emir Amanullah Khan after Anglo-Afghan War in 1839. The inclusion of Pashtuns in the security establishment only became possible after the takeover by General Ayub Khan and General Yahya Khan, both from NWFP, with their numbers further increased by General Ziaul Haq during the "Afghan Jihad" period of the cold war.

Can borders alone decide policies?

Pakistan's foreign policy and strategic vision consists of two basic interconnected factors – inward external security and outward internal concerns defined within the context of its relationship with Afghanistan and India. Historically, Pakistan has worked within the boundaries of alliances with the US, Saudi Arabia, and China, serving international interests that suit the Pakistani civil-military elite, and supports retrogressive Arab nationalism manifested into the extremist Islamist movements. After sixty years of the country's existence, its foreign policy triangle has evolved into a Central Asia – China and Iran axis. Pakistan's security in broader terms is defined by its immediate neighbors and inversely associated with internal concerns and interests, which are ironically defined by a very much non-representative establishment of the country.

A review of Pakistan's border "security concerns" is alarming. The country faces aggression at the upper eastern border of divided Punjab and Kashmir; their desert and costal borders of Sindh with India capitalized by the non-hostile-to-India Sindhi demography; an insurgency in Pakistani and Iranian Balochistan at the western lower borders; a porous borders with Afghanistan; and over its mountainous border with China, there is a continuing insurgency in the Xinjiang province.

Pakistan today is not thinking beyond the creation of a stable Afghanistan with a Pakistan-friendly Pashtuns population. It wrongly believes that the emergence of such a neighbor will minimize security concerns of nationalist resentment in Pashtun populated KPK, Northern Balochistan and Federally Administered Tribal Areas (FATA). Additionally, the Taliban are recognized strategic assets of Pakistan, and Pakistan already has fears of Afghanistan turning into a hostile country after the ISAF withdrawal in 2014.

Statecraft dispositions

These indicators of state crises will only dissipate if Pakistan adopts a paradigm shift in its foreign policy along with extensive reforms in its federal structure and demographic chemistry of the state apparatus.

Fallacies in politics are always counterproductive. That Pashtun strategy is framed on the notion of Talbanization along with the Durand Line has become a paradox. Secular Pashtun political forces within Pakistan are still able to carve out new positive corridors, whilst the Taliban have tactically killed the majority of tribal elders in the KPK to take hold of the area. However, there are many veteran tribal elders in Pakistan with greater ties on the other side of the Durand Line that could be beneficial for the true peace initiatives. This requires 180 degree shift in Pakistan's Afghanistan policy. Strategic blunders like dividing Pashtuns to ensure internal security have already led Pakistan into blind alley. Pakistan needs to support the reconstruction along with reconciliation in Afghanistan; restraining the Taliban; and carrying out reforms and development in the FATA and KPK.

Besides, Pakistan's Afghanistan policy is wrapped with its historic concerns of India, which should now be addressed. If ISAF is withdrawing by 2014 without leaving behind a sovereign capable government in Afghanistan, it may prove to be disastrous for the stability in South Asia. Therefore, political solution is the only passage.
A positive settlement in Afghanistan is only possible when US, India, Iran, Pakistan, Central Asia and China devise a roadmap along with observers like Germany, Turkey and Saudi Arabia for the state building and reconstruction of Afghanistan.

A 180 degree shift in Pakistan's India policy would only be possible if state chemistry in Pakistan is altered. For the introduction of this higher degree strategic shift in its India policy, Pakistan must first address the need for internal reforms within the country such as restructuring its federal system and ensuring all major ethnic groups can participate in statecraft.

The energy needs of Pakistan are pushing it towards Central Asia, Iran, and Eurasia. Without a stable Afghanistan, interaction with these Central Asian States and Eurasia is impossible, and the survival of Pakistan will come primarily from the resolution of intra-state conflicts, federal reforms, the separation of religion from the state, and from providing equal rights to all ethnic and religious minorities. It also requires revisiting the matrix of the state's legitimacy which is based on a two-nation theory; internal stability and security concerns vis-à-vis neighboring countries.

The cost of Pakistan's interventions

Pakistan army overwhelmingly consists of ethnic Punjabis and the Muhajir community. Its engagement in Afghanistan has proved to be highly beneficial for the military as well as civil entrepreneur of Punjab in economic and monetary terms. However, it is Sindh that has paid the price of Pakistan's Afghan interventions, including the war against terror, in the form of the influx of refugees. Sindh, the only secular province of Pakistan, is now also facing the possibility of being "Talbanized" by the security establishment as the supply of ISAF forces and access of land locked Afghanistan to international trade is through Karachi, the capital of Sindh.

Unfortunately, the international community that is engaged in the reconstruction of Afghanistan has never pressurized Pakistan to ensure the federal rights of Sindh province. As a reaction to such an oppressive policy, more than one million people of Sindh marched in the city of Karachi under the banner of "Freedom March 2012" and demanded the international community to intervene for the freedom of Sindh. A similar situation is also happening in Balochistan where the struggle for freedom has been underway since 2002.

The road to transformation

Pakistan's behavior as a state is a reflection of its early state building patterns; an extremely centralized federalism; a demographic hegemony providing for the interests of the dominant Punjab province; ethnic uniformity in the security establishment; a demoralized and fragmented civilian population; the militarization of civil institutions; and a state ideology with the imposition of Saudi Salafism on the Sunni Hanfiya majority.

A paradigm shift in the definition of Pakistani state-doctrine is a prerequisite for the transformation of country. Extensive federal reforms accompanied by demographic and geographic securities for the federal provinces and their historical people with proportionate participation in the security regime and civil bureaucracy are required alongside the liberalization of society. Greater autonomy and authority for the civilian leadership would then become unavoidable, minimizing the Army's role in the leadership of the country.

The transformation into a viable state through federal reforms and restructuring state-doctrine and the paradigm shift in the foreign policy vision are interdependent. Pakistan requires a sociopolitical, federal, and state transformation. If this is not attained, both anarchy and chaos may prevail, threatening a human catastrophe or a situation that will lead to the creation of new break-away sovereign states.

Published in The Descrier, UK www.descrier.co.uk on May 02, 2013

Dynamics of Pakistani Establishment

Pakistan is unpredictable. The two decades long world engagement with Pakistan for the essential reforms in the state-field, society and economy has failed to give results. There is no full stop to the religious extremism as well as its export, anti-democratic moves and extreme centralization of the federal governance.

The internal ground realities of Pakistan has been the epicenter of instability in the neighboring India and Afghanistan; broader insecurity in Central-and-South Asia as well as Middle East. It has risked international interests in Asian geo-strategic regions and to certain extent internal security of the Western Europe, northern America, some African countries, Eurasia, and the East Asian countries including China. Addressing this broader cloud of insecurity would be possible only by understanding and addressing the dynamics of the Pakistan establishment and the state apparatus.

Ethnic dynamism

The fault lines internal and external insecurity run through the ethno-sectarian composition of Pakistan's civil and military Establishment. No ethnic-nation out of Punjabi, Sindhi, Baloch, Pashtun and Siraiki form significant majority in Pakistan; however Punjab, as a province, forms numerical majority. The ethnic minorities are second and third generation of Urdu speaking refugee from India, Hindko linguistic group of Khyber Pakhtunkhuwa (K-P), Persian speaking Hazara of Balochistan and Potohari speaking districts of northeastern Punjab. The peculiarity of the Pakistani federalism is the dominance of ethnic and sectarian minorities over the majority. Hence, the ethno-sectarian minority's hold of Establishment and the State apparatus is the source of internal oppression, discrimination, manipulation and violence and foundation of external policy manifestations.

The military as well as security establishment of Pakistan is dominated by ethnic Punjabi that is majority only in 18 districts out of 36 districts of Punjab province and 106 districts of the country. Majority of soldiers in Pakistan Army are ethno-linguistic Potohari, which are majority only in four northeastern districts of Punjab. Although Potohari are ethno-linguistically separate; however the Urdu medium education in across Punjab and Punjabi majority of non-commissioned and commission officers in the military has virtually converted Potohari into Punjabi to the extent that the Potohari language has vanished. Rest of the ethnic composition of the military is Urdu speaking that form second significant ethnic group among the commissioned officers despite the fact that they are ethnic majority in only one district of Sindh – district Central Karachi – out of 23 districts of the province. Hindko of K-P that are majority in 6 districts out of 25 districts in K-P province and Hazara of Balochistan that does not form majority in any of the 32 district of Balochistan. They have higher participation in the commissioned and non-commissioned officers in the Army proportionate to their population.

Pashtun of K-P and to certain extent Balochistan have participation in the military only because Pakistan borders with Pashtu speaking provinces of Afghanistan. Sindhi and Baloch together would hardly form one percent in the military and bellow one person of the military associated security agencies. Similar trend also dominates the civil and military security and intelligence fraternity.

The pattern of civil establishment is slightly different; however does not break the taboo of ethnic and sectarian minorities' dominance over the rest. Punjabi, Urdu, Hindko and Hazara are given more opportunities in civil bureaucracy against their constitutionally determined share. Punjabi and Urdu are given employment opportunities in civil-bureaucracy out of Sindhi quota in Sindh; Punjabi and Hazara out Baloch quota in Balochistan, Hindko out of Pashtun quota in K-P and Punjabi take out of Sirakis share in Punjab. Electoral governance and the Parliament are also on similar pattern. Punjab province has largest number of seats in the bicameral parliament of Pakistan therefore Sindh, K-P and Balochistan together does not form constitutionally required two-third majority to amend the Constitution of Pakistan.

Sectarian and ideological contours

Sunni is the overwhelming majority of Pakistani Muslim. Shia is the second significant group, whose majority resides in Sindh and Siraiki southern Punjab. Both Sunni and Shia follow the Hanfiya orthodox of Islamic jurisprudence in broader terms. Salafi are below two percent of the total Muslims. Contrary to the social composition of Pakistan, the Establishment upholds and promotes Salafism. Al-Qaida, ideologically, was Salafist. In Pakistan Jamait-e-Islami, Lashkar-e-Jhangvi, and Jamaa't ul Dawa (JuD) which was previously Lashkare-e-Tayyaba (LeT) are leading Salafi outfits. Since Salafis are tiniest sectarian minority among Pakistani Muslims, the Sunni majority usually becomes member of ideologically Salafi religious parties. The leadership of these outfits however remains with Salafis.

Liberal, secular and moderate have are also in significant in the Establishment. Their majority is the second or third generation of Punjabi and Urdu refugees belonged to the pre-1947 Indian provinces in which Muslim were minority and played key role in the 1947 partition of India. Muslim nationhood, minority rule over majority, anti-Hindu, anti-Indian and anti-Afghan tilts are the by-product of this historical background. Internally anti-Christian and externally anti-West, particularly anti-American, policies are the result of Salafi dominancy and Sudaization of Pakistani state. Sufi-secular and liberal Sindh, Balochistan and Siraiki southern Punjab does not suit dominant groups' internal power greed and external dispositions.

External-internal nexus

Ethnic Punjabi and sectarian Salafi dominance on Pakistan in alliance with the other minority ethnicities is the caterpillar of Pakistan's foreign policy and strategic engagements. Therefore, the discrimination and non-inclusion of Sindhi, Baloch, Siraki and to some extent Pashtun in the decision making layers of the establishment is directly proportionate with dominant groups' policy for India, Afghanistan, Iran, USA and EU. At one stage, the ethnicity dominates the sects, because Pakistan's military has a history of Christian and Ahmadiya Muslim Generals. On the other hand, no Sindhi Muslim has been promoted even to the post of

Brigadier General; however only one Baloch was promoted Lt. General, who was retired prematurely against his seniority of qualifying the post of Army Chief after Musharaf.

Reforms versus Revolution There are only two options for Pakistan and the interested world: (i) undertaking higher scale reforms in the Pakistan establishment in the ethnic, sectarian, religious and ideological perspective or (ii) materialization of Sindhi and Baloch peoples' demanded for the independent and sovereign statehood. Practically, the later is more possible than the earlier since perversion has reached the level of irreversibility.

Published in Daily Afghanistan Times, September 4, 2014

Pakistan Policy of USA

America is changing. The impression of 'changing America' is widely traveling these days in Southern Pakistan, the culturally Sufi-secular belt of the ancient Indus civilization. Tens of millions Sindhi, Baloch and Siraiki receive this changing America notion auspiciously. This, to them, is the policy and the engagement framework changes that promise bolstering their politics, culture and tradition deeply rooted in tolerant diversity. In recent past, particularly during mid-eighties, the very same people were against US policies of supporting military regime of General Zia, who overthrew the elected government of Zulfiqar Ali Bhutto and hanged him.

In fact, the USA-Pakistan relations have ascertained particular limelight in the post nine-eleven discourse on Iraq and Afghanistan. Political analysts and strategists, hitherto, have tried to see these relations in the context of ongoing war against terrorism. What impacts the US-Pak relations have left on the state-building, socio-political fabric and ethnic composite of the power? And, what are the contemporary contours of it? A domain that is almost untouched as yet.

An era of new strategic possibilities for the world powers began with the creation of Pakistan out of undivided India on August 14, 1947. The new country was formed on the basis of Indian Muslim nationhood. It became a federation of Muslim majority states of Indus civilization, and the state of East Bengal, which is now Bangladesh. Despite the fact that Sindh, Balochistan and NWFP (now Khyber Pakhtunkhuwa) province rejected the very idea of Pakistan during the Indian provincial elections of 1946, the emergence of Pakistan became inevitable due to unexplained reason by the British colonizers against the will of Baloch and

Sindh to remain independent countries as they were before 1843 invasion by Britain. This will was instrumented through 1946 elections.

The creation of Pakistan lured the cold war rivals Union of Soviet Socialist Republics (USSR) and United States of America (USA). USSR was the first country to invite Pakistani Prime Minister; however Prime Minister Liaqat Ali Khan postponed its USSR visit due to sudden invitation by USA. Thus, the USA-Pakistan relation incepted with the bottom line of anti-USSR. This laid foundations of Pakistan's prolonged role in the cold war against USSR.

State-building, military and governance

Being bordered with USSR neighboring Afghanistan as well as China and India, Pakistan's geo-strategic importance led it to become a frontline blaze in the capitalist-socialist tug of war in Afghanistan. The ambits of cold war were so high that world did not bother to give a deep insight into its internal socio-political and state chemistry of Pakistan before coming into the military, strategic and political partnership.

Since Pakistan was created against the will of Sindhi, Baloch, Pashtun and Siraiki Muslim and Hindu, they were kept away from the state-affairs. M. A. Jinnah, the founding father of the country, was a Sindhi who died in one year after the creation of Pakistan. The Indian partition of 1947 was not only partition of land, but also of the human resources. The Punjabi Muslims of Indian Army and Urdu speaking northern Indian Muslim bureaucracy, as a partition of human resources, were handed over to the newly found State of Pakistan to run the country. This harbored permanent dominancy of the few non-indigenous ethnic groups over the rest. Until now, no indigenous person from eastern provinces of Sindh and Punjab has been promoted to the post of Brigadier General in Pakistan Army. Only one Baloch and bellow a dozen Pashtun Generals have led Pakistan's politically strong military. The army mainly is comprised of ethnic Punjabi, with a smaller participation of Pashtun, as well as Urdu speaking community who refuge mainly in Sindh from today's India after 1947 partition riots.

The cold war military and strategic support to Pakistan, no doubt, facilitated the West in Afghan war against USSR; however it resulted into an internal antagonism within Pakistan through patronization of Punjabi dominance. It was a kind of internal-colonialism through which the establishment of Pakistan kept on exploiting the natural and economic resources of Sindh and Balochistan for the benefit of Punjab province.

The active partnership in USA led international political and strategic alliance, gave Pakistan Army a cushion to over-power the internal governance in the country due to which it took over the country's power for nearly three decades. The military also hanged highly popular Prime Minister Zulfiqar Ali Bhutto, and allegedly managed the murder of his daughter Benazir Bhutto. No civil government, except the President Zardari's (2008-20013), could complete the constitutional tenure in sixty-seven years history.

Talbanization & Pseudo-Islam

Taliban are the barbaric terrorists who blend and brandish terrorism with Islam. They are a criminal by-product of the Jihadist machinery that was found in 1980-1981 to wage a proxy war against USSR in Afghanistan. After dismemberment of USSR, USA and its allies quit Afghan war-field, leaving the weapons and militant Mullahs behind for Pakistan. Pakistan kept on using them as their strategic tools to occupy Afghanistan.

Taliban took over Afghanistan and ruled it against the will and culture of Afghan people until USA ousted them from Afghanistan after nine-eleven. Religious extremism changed the socio-cultural fabric of Afghan society from Afghan Sufi Muslims historically in harmony with Buddhism and Hinduism into violent Salafism – a so-called sect of Islam which in fact is against the very essence of Islamic education. Pakistan's military establishment today is using the same tactics against USA which it has learnt from it during the anti-soviet campaign in Afghanistan; however the cost of which is being paid by the non-Punjabi population of Sindh, Balochistan and Khyber Pakhtunkhuwa province, which still are the cultural upholders of secular and diversified civilization of Indus. Sindh being cradle of Indus civilization is the only secular province in Pakistan, which fights back against religious intolerance.

Extremist Mullahs, today, are being unleashed and their seminaries are being widely opened in Sindh, Balochistan, and South Punjab that together form culturally liberal and Sufi belts of South Asia. This is an attempt to permanently convert the Indus plains and hills into future's Salafi terror dens on the lines of ISIS in Iraq. According to the Declan Walsh story in the New York

Times, the Salafi outfit Lashkar-e-Jhangvi that has been an ally of Al-Qaida has gradually been increasing its presence in these provinces. This not only pose threat to the historically Sufi-secular traits of Sindhi and Baloch culture, but also is meant to resist freedom movements in Sindh and Balochistan, and probably is a preparation to give further checkmate to USA-India in the changing regional strategic scenario.

Crimes against humanity

Tens of thousands have been killed so far in Pakistan during last fifteen years either by the state supported militant groups or by the state agencies including the military, second-tier armed forces, police and the intelligence outfits like Inter Services Intelligence (ISI) and Military Intelligence (MI). A vast number of Sindhi Hindus have been virtually forced to leave their ancestral homeland and refuge into India, whose number has crossed one hundred thousand over the decade. The military and intelligence technology it acquired from USA earlier during 1965-1988 and later on during General Musharaf's regime in 2000s was mainly used to counter the freedom war in Balochistan and peaceful freedom mass movement in Sindh.

A futuristic US policy

The experience of the ethnic non-Punjabi people of Pakistan, international community and the South Asian nations and most importantly of the USA foretells that USA not only should revise its foreign policy engagement with Pakistan at the level one-eighty degree but also in the humanistic interests of the Sindhi, Baloch, Siraiki and Pashtun people, who not only form majority population of Pakistan but also are culturally liberal. This is also required for giving a full stop to the ethnic cleansing of Sindhi and Baloch and economic exploitation of Sindh and Balochistan that together house the largest natural resources reservoirs of oil, natural gas, coal and gold in South Asia. Besides, US should also reconsider its cordial relations with the organizations like Mutahida Qaumi Movement (MQM), a party that's hell-bent on dividing Sindh. Moreover, the freedom movements in Sindh and Balochistan are secular therefore they are the only viable force to counter growing state-sponsored Muslim extremism within and outside Pakistan.

Daily Afghanistan Times, Sep 22, 2014

COLONIAL STRINGS OF INTERNAL EXPLOITATION

Why Britain is responsible to the people of Sindh and Balochistan

Scottish people decide their political future according to their will. No doubt it is political civilization of UK due to which it agreed with the Parliament of Scotland for holding a referendum of the union versus secession. It is an important moment when UK also needs to consider its obligations for the political morality concerning its previous colonies.

The previous British colonies are globally in the media lime light today. Conflicts, violence and wars have become commonplace in the regions that were colonized by Great Britain between the seventeenth and nineteenth centuries.

Why after winning freedom in the wake of Second World War, the previous British colonies in Asia are still yearning for the real freedoms, development, peace and human security? The answer can only be found in the design and modus operandi of the colonial rule as well as the Britain's departure strategy from the colonies after 1945. One cannot underestimate, however, the positive contribution of the Britain imperialism of putting the modern foundations of state-building, development and social-transformation in the colonies, which earlier were unable to transform from feudal societies and barter economies into the Industrial and modern one.

South Asia is a highly intelligible and comprehensive example of the prolonged instability among the previous British colonies despite the fact that Iraq and Kuwait in the Middle East have been centre-stage of world politics of conflicts during the last three decades. The partition of Kuwait from the historical Iraqi territory had arguably lesser impacts on the Asian politics of the international interests than that of the partition of the Indian Subcontinent due to South-and-Central Asian strategic contours.

This is important to note that like Pakistan there has been no country named 'Iraq' in the history; neither the contemporary Iraqi geography has ever been a sovereign country.

Sri Lanka, Myanmar, Pakistan and Bangladesh have undergone several waves of conflicts, violence, civil rights violations and crimes against humanity, militarization and the wars in the post-colonial era. Mainland India alone has socio-politically elevated to certain extent from such broader instability.

Among South Asian countries, Pakistan is a peculiar case study of the inappropriate, unrealistic and unjustified designs of the Imperial Britain, which have resulted into the broader insecurity for the tens of millions Sindhi, Baloch and Pashtun. The colonial and contemporary unrealistic experiences of the world community with the internal politics of Pakistani ethno-national dynamics have damaged both Sindhi-Baloch-Pashtun and the international community.

Rationality behind Pakistan and the realities

No historian, academician or analyst has hitherto found an appropriate rationale for creating Pakistan. The historical documents note that Pakistan was created on the line of so-called two-nation theory based on Indian Hindu and Muslim nationhood. The idea of Pakistan was rejected by the federating provinces of Sindh, Balochistan, and NWFP (now Khyber Pakhtunkhuwa - KPK), and Siraiki speaking people of Southern Punjab that together form roughly ninety percent of geography and seventy percent of the population of Pakistan.

The founding political party of Pakistan, the All India Muslim League (AIML), never won elections in British India from Sindh and KPK and did not win contested elections in Balochistan. The Siraiki people of today's South Punjab were already in historical conflict with Ranjit Singh's Punjab and were autonomous and sovereign princely territories before the British invasion of Punjab. It was only East Bengal (now Bangladesh), where the AIML was not only founded in 1906, but also won the elections later on in 1946. If the composition of AIML's Central Working Committee (CWC) is reviewed, one finds that only one Sindhi leader M. A. Jinnah was part of it, who in fact resigned from the Indian National Congress (INC) in 1913 due to personal reasons. The rest of AIML's leadership was from Northern India, especially from the pre-partition United Provinces (UP) of India that today form the Utter Pradesh, Bihar and Utrankhand states of India; Delhi, Punjab (today Indian Punjab), the Central Provinces (CP) comprising today's Madhya Pradesh and Andhra Pradesh states, and the East Bengal. There was no Baloch or Pashtun member of AIML's CWC.

Pakistan was demanded by the population and leadership of the undivided Indian provinces / states that today do not form Pakistan. Since Sindhi, Baloch, Pashtun and Siraiki Muslims formed majorities in their historical motherlands; their interests were secure and almost unchallenged within undivided India. Pakistan was demanded by the Muslim minority population and their aristocrat leadership from UP, CP and today's Indian Punjab. Therefore, the creation of Pakistan by clubbing together states that were against the very idea of Pakistan was a historical blunder committed by the colonial British rulers against the will of the people.

After Indian partition in 1947, the state of Pakistan was taken over by those who migrated from Muslim minority provinces of undivided India and settled into newly formed Pakistan. Thus, the non-indigenous peoples' control of the state apparatus transformed the Pakistani state into an anti-indigenous people, particularly against the interests of indigenous ethnic-nations. Like today, the Indian power historically has been led by the northern India. No historical document narrates the movements and struggles by the South Indian people of undivided India. Hence, the partition of India was not only against the will of the federating provinces of today's Pakistan but also did not include the consultation and opinion of the South Indian provinces. It is therefore logically reached that the partition of India was a result of the conflict between northern Indian Muslims, who were aristocrat, and Hindu, who were industrialists and traders over the political and economic power; however the conflict was mostly fostered by the British colonialism to prolong their rule in India.

The extreme-communal mindset of AIML leadership at the time of partition was worth notable especially from the case of Punjabi Sikh community. When the question of Punjab partition arose, the Sikhs were asked to choose between India and Pakistan. They preferred unity of Punjab, and for achieving that they were ready to live in either country for the sake of it. They also considered the option of Pakistan, according to historical documents, because the birth place of their religious messenger Guru Nanak was falling in the proposed Pakistani parts of Punjab; however the AIML leadership rejected the very notion of housing non-Muslims into the land of Muslims. The division of Punjab was painful for Sikh at the time of partition; however the history of victimization of religious minorities in Pakistan have given them a feeling of security and prosperous in India.

Hindu Maha Sabha, Sindh League, Sindh United Party, Unionist Party of Punjab, Sindh Sagar Party, Hur Jam'at (Sindhi), Azad Hind Army, NWFP Congress and Parliament of the autonomous Balochistan were against the partition of India. Rest of the Indian political parties including Communist Party of India as well as the top communist ideologue and philosopher M. N. Roy, an Asian member of Communist International (CommIntern) were also in the favor of Indian partition since.

Sovereign Sindh and Balochistan

Sindh and Balochistan have thousands years history of sovereign countries. They together have also remained one country in the earlier part of their history as a Kingdom of Sindh; however later on they became separate independent and sovereign countries of Sindh and Khanate of Kalat (Balochistan). British invaded sovereign Sindh in 1843 and Balochistan and 1854 in bid to invade Afghanistan. Before their invasion of Sindh-Balochistan, more than a dozen treaties were signed between sovereign country of Sindh and the Great Britain as well as at least one major treaty was signed between the sovereign country of Khanate of Kalat and the Great Britain. According to these treaties, Britain ensured Sindh and Balochistan that it would not invade them; rather protect them, if both open-up river Indus and the route to Kandahar in Afghanistan. British violated its own treaties twice – once when it occupied both by the mid eighties and later in 1947 (Sindh) and 1948 (Balochistan) when both were annexed to Pakistan against the will of the people. British also held treaties with the Siraiki sovereign state of Bahwalpur in 1833 ensuring them protection from the invasion of Ranjit Singh's Punjab. Bahawalpur State and other Siraiki districts, against the sprit of 1833 treaty, were annexed to Pakistani Punjab after 1947.

In fact Sindh waged four wars against British invasion and colonialism in 1843, 1843-1857, 1890-1899 and finally in 1940-1943. In the last war against colonial rule, at least twenty thousand Sindhi combatants, known as Hurs, were killed by British Army and Air Force, and thousands of Sindhi families were sent to concentration camps in Sindh, Rajasthan and Bengal. The freedom war leader Pir Pagara Soriyah Badshah was hanged and his burial place was concealed, which still stands unknown to the Sindhi people. Some Sindhi freedom fighters and guerrilla commanders were hanged, and a large number of them were kept in prisons of Pakistan by the Pakistani authorities until 1965, even after the eighteen years of British departure from Indian Subcontinent.

UK and internal colonialism in Pakistan

Although British departed from Indian Subcontinent (India, Pakistan and Bangladesh) in 1947, it kept its strategic strings attached with Pakistani establishment. United States of America (USA) partnered with Pakistan later on. Pakistan, which was created on the basis of so-called two-nation theory of Indian Muslim-nationhood, broke-up in 1971 on the lines of Bengali ethnic-nationhood after the military committed heinous crimes against humanity of killing and raping hundreds of thousands Bengalis. Pakistan authorities were not even appropriately criticized by the international community against such a brutality. The 1971 break-up of Pakistan on the basis of ethno-national grounds invalidated the 'Two-nation theory' and thus shaken the ideological basis of Pakistan on which it was created by the Britain.

The British connections with the Punjabi dominated Pakistani establishment, partnered by the Urdu speaking northern Indian refugees in Sindh are still of great importance. This is phenomenal from the fact that the largest outward migrations from Pakistan have been of ethnic Punjabi, majority of which have preferred to settle into previous British colonies as well dominion states especially UK, Canada and Australia. Punjabi, particularly Muslim Punjabi, forms significant immigrated population of UK, and are the majority of Vanccour in Canada. The current Governor of Punjab in Pakistan, Muhammad Sarwar, was the first generation immigrant Punjabi who did not only become a Parliamentarian in UK but also was the Deputy Leader of the House in Scottish Parliament. He has migrated back to Pakistan in 2013 after resigning his Parliamentarian seat in UK and became Governor of Punjab within one month of settling back in Pakistan. Despite the fact that ethnic Sindhi are the largest South Asian contributors of the UK economy, they have never remained on the priority of British engagement within Pakistan. Even the non-indigenous leadership of the racial political group like MQM from Pakistan has been given support in UK, who still seems to be stuck on the division of Sindh.

During the sixty-seven years partnership of UK and US in Pakistan, especially their engagement in Afghanistan in the proxy war against USSR, both have been favoring Punjabis and strengthened Punjabi dominated Pakistan Army on the cost of ethnic-nations Sindhi, Baloch, Pashtun and Siraiki.

Sindh is the largest economic contributor of Pakistan. Balochistan and Sindh together form the natural resource richest belt in South Asia. Pakistani establishment that is pre-dominantly Punjabi has developed Punjab and Punjabi dominated military on the resources as well as at the cost of Sindh and Balochistan. Thousands have been killed in both of the provinces in last three decades by the armed forces. A highly massive freedom movement is going on in Sindh, which gathered more than five million Sindhis in Karachi on March 23, 2014 and demanded the international community's intervention for the freedom of Sindh.

There is also an armed struggle in Sindh; however it has never attacked a human target. Meanwhile, Baloch are waging a full scale freedom war in Balochistan since 1999 against the occupation of Punjab. Crimes against humanity, genocides and ethnic cleansing have alarmed the people of conscience around the globe.

Possible role of the UK

UK, being successor of the Great Britain, is historically responsible for the ill-designs and mishaps it has committed while departing from the colonies after the Second World War. It should feel more responsible to the oppressed nations in Pakistan whom British invaded as independent and sovereign countries and later on annexed them with the Pakistan against their will. British should also revise its policies and engagement within Pakistan and think undoing the blunders it has committed during 1947 and later on, whose cost is being paid by the Sindhi, Baloch, Pashtun and Siraiki people in Pakistan.

Daily Afghanistan Times, Sep 18, 2014

Decolonizing Development

The politics of international development has never asserted its hitherto potential role to address changes in development paradigms, rights regimes and social movements in internally colonized countries across the globe. Pakistan, in this regard, could be the first-ever model for this kind of a new initiative.

What role can developed countries like the United States, the United Kingdom and Canada together possibly play in some crucial issues of Pakistan? One may probably dismiss the very notion by terming it irrelevant; however, realpolitik sometimes precedes the theoretical matrix. In fact, the politics of international development has much to offer for development decolonization in internally colonized countries.

The US, UK, and Canada indeed have a highly peculiar and candid engagement with Pakistan due to various reasons. They are allies in the Afghanistan intervention. They headquarter a highly vibrant Christian missionary in the Punjab and Sindh provinces. Additionally, they house powerful Pakistani Punjabi elite in cities like Vancouver, London and Staten Island in New York. These three cities have played a major role in lobbying for Pakistan's Punjabi-dominated military establishment. Very few within and outside of Pakistan know the crucially important, diplomatic role these cities have due their degree of influence in Pakistan's internal politics. The US, UK, and Canada are among the top five donors in the development and rights regime in Pakistan, where the largest amount of civil society actors is outcome of, as well as associated with, CIDA, DFID and USAID.

Opposites in similarities

If a wider range of socio-political and strategic facts is taken into account regarding the American, Britain and Canadian niche for economic and financial assistance in Pakistan, the restructuring of such an intervention on ethno-demographic segregation becomes an inevitable prerequisite. This will ultimately have highly progressive effects if other stakeholders like Germany, Russia, India and Japan join in such a noble task.

In the wider range of global politics, Canada hitherto has postured itself as a soft ally of the US and the UK has been an old ally since the Cold War. The UK is a previous colonizer who morally holds greater responsibilities for whatever is happening in Pakistan due its inappropriate and haphazard departure from Pakistan. Moreover, the nature of relations between Canada, US, and the UK as well as the Canadian passion for an enhanced role in global politics further pitches her for revisiting the Pakistan policy.

From the immigration-demographic standpoint, these countries have two edges for their possible role regarding the much required 180-degree reform in Pakistan. Moreover, the UK and Canada have classical similarities as well concerning the dissent between states and the federal government. In the UK, Scotland has its own currency—the Scottish Pound—and a referendum for its cessation was already due. (which finally held, and Scottish people chose union over cessession) Meanwhile Canada has been appropriately addressing the issue of Quebec, for which they held a referendum. Unlike the UK and Canada, Pakistan has been unsuccessful in addressing similar popular demands from Sindh and Balochistan in a democratic and judicious manner. In fact, these freedom movements in Pakistan have been unfortunately handled through a brutal, undemocratic and unethical use of military power against the citizenry.

The United Kingdom, Canada, and the US house some of the largest populations of Pakistani Punjabis; thus, it becomes relevant for their foreign policies to include the chemistry change in the Pakistani power matrix and statecraft through development intervention policies.

Non-inclusive matrix

There can be a strong role for the US, UK, and Canada in overhauling Pakistan statecraft in association with some Western and South Asian stakeholders for the country's real substantive democratization, which may leave positive impacts on the desperately required state chemistry change. It is now a well-discussed fact among analysts that the state apparatus of Pakistan is non-inclusive unto its very foundations by being confined only to the ethnic Punjabis, mostly of Salafi Muslim origin. The rest of the citizens, especially the Sindhis and Balochs and religious groups like Hindus, Christians and Shia Muslims, are officially or traditionally barred from strategic positions, like the heads of the armed forces. Additionally, non-Muslims are constitutionally discriminated against by being denied their right to hold the public offices of the President and the Prime Minister.

Although there is no constitutional bar on Sindhis and Balochs for the top positions, the practical norms are otherwise. No Sindhi military official has so far been promoted to the post of Brigadier General. Moreover, only one Baloch general has hitherto succeeded to the senior rank who, during Musharaf's military regime, also qualified for the post of Deputy Army Chief. However, he was asked to retire prematurely.

Quite surprisingly, for civil society organizations, international development funds flow, and private entrepreneur recruitment, including for multi-national companies, usually practice ethnic bias in Pakistan because the majority of these house ethnic Punjabi employees in senior and mid-level management. Even in the oil and gas-rich province of Sindh, hardly any Sindhi can be found in technical and non-technical positions for officers and laborers.

Federative dissent

Due to the *Punjabization* of the state apparatus in Pakistan, in association with its Urdu-speaking elite partners, Bangladesh waged and won a war for freedom in 1971. Balochistan has been waging a liberation war for the last couple of decades and Sindh is leading a peaceful movement where a couple of million people demanded independence in 2012. Recently around five million Sindhis gathered in the Karachi city on March 23, 2014 to demand that the United Nations and the world community intervene for an 'Independent Sindh'. At least two top leaders, Bashir Qureshi and Maqsood Qureshi, have been killed in Sindh during the last two years, besides the extra-judicial murder of hundreds of Sindhi and Baloch political and human rights activists and journalists. More than 10,000 activists, roughly estimating, were involuntarily disappeared from both the southern coastal and natural resource rich provinces of Sindh and Balochistan. Recently, numerous mass graves have been found, according to news reports from various parts of Balochistan, indicating war crimes committed during the conflict between the military and the Baloch rebels.

A crucial engagement

While South Asian countries need to be concerned about happenings in their immediate neighborhood, developed countries like the US, Canada, the UK, Russia and Japan can play at least one basic yet crucial three-pronged role in Pakistan. One, they can review their foreign policy and international development priorities in the socio-political context and prioritize issues like 'ethno-sectarian participation' in governance as well as human rights support in the context of political, economic and culture rights to Sindh and Balochistan provinces. Two, they can push Pakistan along with other stakeholders to hold a referendum in a democratic manner in Sindh and Balochistan, similar to Canada and the UK's plans to do so in Quebec and Scotland, respectively. Three, where Punjabi-speaking Pakistani settlers in the US, UK and Canada have played a major role in Islamabad's politics and diplomacy, the time has come for the American, Canadian and British Sindhi and Baloch Diaspora to also be encouraged for a progressive role in the state chemistry and a rights regime change in Pakistan. Most importantly, native Western activists can at least show their activism sympathy for the victims of ethnic cleansing, genocide and rights violation in Sindh and Balochistan.

Let development equality be reinforced to strengthen social justice and peace for a better tomorrow.

Published in Daily The Kathmandu Post on May 04, 2014

Colonized Internally

The boom of socialist politics in the global order between 1950-1970s, the Cold War episode that played out in Afghanistan during the 1980s and the 'war on terror' during the 2000s have been instrumental in state development, social progress, economic growth and the political narrative of Southasia. These global conflicts for power and resources have always been an external factor behind the gap in between states and societies.

After the British withdrawal, Southasian states needed a new state apparatus as the old ones were built to serve the interests of external colonizers. But the continuation of the colonial legacy of the state apparatus created local and internal colonizers who preferred to collaborate with external post-colonial and neo-colonial elements instead of redirecting progress and development to the people.

Due to the much-touted contest between the so-called socialist and capitalist blocks during the 1950-80s, the governments in India, Pakistan, Sri Lanka, Myanmar, Nepal, Bhutan and the Maldives could not bridge the gaps between the state and society by transforming the colonial, aristocratic and monarchial natures of their respective state oligarchies into a localized one.

Internal colonization

In some of the previous colonies in Asia and Africa, the withdrawal of colonizers created an ethno-linguistic, racial, and/or sectarian hegemony and oligarchy over the rest of the citizenry, especially by transferring state powers to selective or loyal ethno-linguistic and religious groups. South Africa, Indonesia and Pakistan have been typical examples of this.

A federation of previously sovereign and independent countries, Pakistan is a typical case study for internally colonized states. State formation in Pakistan has been a classic hegemony of ethnic

Punjabis in association with the cultural, political and economic partnership of the Urdu-speaking elite over the rest of the federated provinces. Due to the Punjabization of Pakistan's military, civil, non-governmental and non-state elements of power, East Pakistan waged a freedom war and emerged as Bangladesh on the world map.

The Pakistani state had tried to accommodate a thin margin of Pashtuns in anti-Soviet campaigns with the support of the US. And it has internally colonized Sindh and Balochistan by accommodating the Urdu ethnic minority in Karachi city. This has resulted in a popular liberation movement, a low intensity insurgency in Sindh and highly intense warfare in Balochistan provinces. It is worth mentioning here that Sindh is the richest land in Southasia in terms of natural resources like oil, coal and methane gas.

Contemporary discontent

Globalization has attached virtual wings to the state apparatus across the globe to fly uninterrupted in comparison to society. It has undermined the previous discourse of the gradual reduction in the role of state in societal affairs.

Technological advancements associated with global connectivity have limited the domain of individual liberties, privacy and movements within and across the nation-states. The worst impact of today's state-oriented globalization, in association with the globalised security doctrines and practices combined with the widening state-society gap, has been pushing the previous colonies to choose between orderly anarchy and result-oriented social movements and transformation.

In fact, the state structures in the previous colonies have become extra-ordinarily advanced and globalised in comparison to their own societies. This phenomenon is exclusive in locally-colonized federations, where federating states/provinces and their ethnic-nations are at odds with the centre or the dominant ethnic groups.

The technology transfer to Pakistan by the West during the last four decades has been misused for the ethnic cleansing of Sindhis and Balochs. The recent unearthing of mass graves in Balochistan and extra-judicial killings in Sindh by security agencies are highly visible evidences of such misuse. It is roughly estimated that the state, as well as state-sponsored mullahs and urban terrorists, have killed around 50,000 commoners so far in Sindh and Balochistan since 2000.

Global linkages

The states of the previous colonies are becoming highly intolerant of social movements, overall rights regimes and individual liberties. The persecution of human rights activists and journalists, the censorship of movies and books, disallowing urban life, limiting freedom for women, attempting to accommodate social movements through structural transformation into failed models are some of the most notable examples. The worst situation can be observed in internally-colonized federations like Pakistan.

Since the people of these countries are in a dilemma of a peculiar kind, in which previous colonizers and neo-imperialists have played key roles, it is necessary that the people from previous colonial and neo-colonial powers come together to raise issues of common concern.

Perversion, dictatorships, local colonies and unnecessary interference of the state apparatus in societies have wrecked havoc in countries like Pakistan.

The time has come for the people of Commonwealth states, of the US and Europe in particular, to step up for real liberation and the development of people in the previous colonies so that states are kept in legitimate brackets, like in countries such as Pakistan.

It is strange that social movements, political rights and civil liberties of the developed and global north societies are highly dependent on the liberation and political salvation of societies in the previous colonies and the Global South. Let the people of previous colonies, particularly internal colonies like Sindh and Balochistan be given moral support in their battle for justice. Proper understanding, will and passion is all that is required to create connectivity for the collectivism of efforts to promote justice.

Besides, studies concerning social movements and civil liberties also need to focus on the process of social-waves versus the structurization of human institutions. No phenomena in the human history of social progress and spiritual development combined with the relation between 'Being' (man) and 'Absolute Being' (nature) have surpassed this fundamental dynamics of human development.

Let us work out the dialectics of humanism for a better harvest of global citizenry, including poor classes and nations in chains around the world.

Published in Daily The Katmandu Post, Nepal on March 30, 2014

Of State and Society

Human society has two inherent permanent features and tendencies—the emergence of social-waves and the process of structuralization in those social-waves. This opposition is a chain of causalities, containing the manifestation of dynamics in the political economy and social progress, as well as their retrogression and social stagnation. No phenomenon of social movements around the globe, particularly in the previous colonies, is an exception to this dialectic of mass expression.

State versus society

Human history has witnessed and undergone this process through the structuralization of movements, religions, ideologies and revolutions. It has left long-lasting imprints on social institutions, particularly the mega-social organism of the state, and on the process of state building and state formation.

The contemporary crises of state versus society and the liberty of the individual versus the state's reckless vigilance using the excuse of national security have deep roots in this fundamental dynamic and dialectic of broader social behavior.

The widening gap between states and societies during the process of globalization is at a highly naïve stage in developed countries, if compared with the developing and underdeveloped world. In other words, state-society frictions in the global north and south have not only their own peculiarities but also variant degrees and velocities of social processes. This is further visible in the polar opposite nature of statehood between the previous colonies and their colonizers.

Besides, on the debris of the state apparatus in previous colonies and colonizers, there have emerged the contemporary virtual forms of soft-colonization, which no doubt is at the height of neo-colonialism and semi-colonialism. This has highly peculiar connotations in ethno-linguistically diverse societies, countries and their arc of class-cum-federal structures.

The impacts of colonization on the polity, state-building and state-society relations in previous colonies and their colonizers are evident. Today's virtual colonialism has even worse aspects to this. Thus, the understanding of state-society relations in the global south, particularly in the previous colonies, in the perspective of contemporary politics and social movement would lead to another stage of discourse. Nevertheless, an analysis of the contemporary state-society relations would hardly re-direct to the hidden depths if the 'structuralism' versus 'social-wave' dynamics is not at the core of broader discourse.

Almost all religions, practical manifestations of political doctrines, movements, and cultural ethos become dogma once swamped in structuralization. The institutions of mullahism, priesthood and panditism, political leadership cults, party dictatorship and thinking stereotypes are common examples.

Colonial state formation

State building and state formation are two different aspects of statehood. State building is a process in which the state evolves out of society through gradual evolution whilst state formation is a process where state construction takes place in a non-traditional manner, based mostly on an extraordinary centralized statehood. State formation in most cases involves the role of external factors in the embryology of the state apparatus.

In the process of state formation, peculiar courses of political actions take place, where particular state elements acquire bigger roles or powers (non-traditionally, if not abnormally) in comparison with others in statecraft.

The formation of a colonial state has historically been aimed at providing a buffer between the colonizers and their subjects. This was attained through creating a class of bureaucrats, sallariat (salaried middle class) and the establishment of various forms of rural-lordships.

The contribution of colonizers in terms of political discourse and culture has helped colonial societies to grow. However, it has meant to regulate relations between colonizers and colonies, mostly in the colonizer's interest. This led, for example, to the previous British colonies wearing a new sociality—a reversal of the previous socio-economic relations. Undivided India is a highly intelligible model of studies for that. India underwent social engineering by the British Raj, which created permanent frictions and upheavals, despite the fact that these are at the heart of development dynamics in South Asia.

The legacy of colonialism has sprung a new course of socio-political metabolism. The independence of colonies, therefore, have gradually and continuously undergone the process of the post-colonial state versus society, the neo-colonial state versus society and internal-colonial or semi-colonial state versus native or internal semi-colonies.

Freedom and the state

If post-British withdrawal from Southasia is deeply analyzed, it will show a peculiar course of state-formation, social progress and consequently, state society conflicts.

If seen in the post-British withdrawal context, various states have undergone an exclusive path to contain the state's classical role of maintaining minimum civil conditions for the citizenry to avail of a free and peaceful life. In so many manners, the state's legitimacy over the use of violence has either been over-used, as in Myanmar and Sri Lanka, or this legitimacy has been shared with state-sponsored extremists, as with the urban terrorists in Pakistan.

The exclusive takeover of the polity and the state apparatus by the particular classes of India after 1947 still carries the strings of colonial statehood, if seen in a state-society perspective. Pakistan has undergone an uneven course of militarization of the state as well as some selective societal groups. Sri Lanka has taken various courses of state retrogression in which state-society relations have been antagonized through a repressive order where harmony has been compromised over the prioritization of the ethnic interest between the Tamil and Sinhala people.

Besides, the state has translated itself gradually into militarization, where minimum civil conditions have always been at the stake. Even Nepal, always proud for never being colonized, has remained under a virtual colonial status since the British occupation of India. Myanmar has become the worst example of a military's dominance over the state apparatus, which turned society retrogressive. Bhutan, like Nepal, is facing the drawbacks of being a land-locked geo-political entity. Maldives, and to certain extent Nepal and Bhutan, has turned itself into a state of convenience in terms of its foreign policy, which ultimately has fall-outs in its own societies and the interests of friendly neighbors. Bangladesh, unlike others, has started cleansing house to detach the impacts, adversaries and strings of Muslim terrorism and war crimes committed by Pakistan in 1971.

Southasian states, naturally, underwent the process of transition after independence from British rule. The state apparatus left behind by the British as an institutional legacy was not only a Southasian adaptation of the Western statehood of its time but was also structured to serve colonial interests and prolong colonial rule. The unexpected withdrawal of the British from Southasia due to World War II left no room to transform the nature of the state apparatus from colonization into a real republic.

The states in Southasia are still structured to serve global powers, in comparison with the interests of their own citizens. In the absence of 'real' colonizers, the role of colonizers has been taken over by civil and military elites. This has squared the level of alienation among the people vis-à-vis the state.

Since most Southasian countries constitute a united diversity, they are reluctant for social movements that lead to a transformation of the state and for the judicious distribution of power vertically and horizontally. Empowerment and development in Southasia is, therefore, conditioned on the judicious distribution of power among ethnicities, classes, communities and sects. Besides, the colonizer's leftover state apparatus legacy is the major reason behind the unending conflicts, underdevelopment and militarization in the region.

If summed up, the transition of Southasian states from colonial into postcolonial states, neocolonial arrangements and semi-colonial as well as internal colonial states has always been the fault on which politics and development in Southasia has been directed and redirected through certain classes, portions of the states apparatus, elitist mindset and structural cultures of the state-society dynamics.

Published in Daily The Kathmandu Post, Nepal on March 03, 2014

Peace beyond Kashmir

Politics in Pakistan has some basic state-ideological, political morality and country-hood fault lines that, in terms of statecraft, are at the helm of almost all internal political catastrophes as well as regional instabilities.

The basic laws of motion in the dynamics of possible change in Pakistan through the futurological view ultimately depend on the country's external engagements, and vice-versa. Peace and the people's security as well as sovereignty within the fragile Pakistani statehood and in South Asia is the greatest concern of our times, especially when this most volatile geo-strategic region houses the nuclear capable Islamic republic, which is sitting on a time bomb of extremism. Pakistan needs to appropriately think, assess and adopt unavoidable political as well as statecraft actions and reforms if it seriously wants to avoid state-failure. The same also applies to its neighborhood, as allies' vis-à-vis their engagement and interests with Pakistan.

Fault lines of political systems

India and Pakistan carried forward colonial political systems after the partition of India in 1947 by continuing with the centralized institution of the Governor General as head of state. However, it was later replaced with the institution of the Presidency. In the context of the political system, the existence of Presidents and Prime Ministers is obvious in countries where the state-society gap—and to a certain extent, antagonism—is highly visible. Nevertheless, positive alterations have also been made; for example in India, by confining Presidencies to ceremonial state leadership.

Establishments in previous Asian colonies mostly have the internal security environment of state-society antagonism. It is at this point that the people's security is compromised by non-participatory establishments in the name of the nation-state security paradigm, which prioritizes geography over people.

It is only with the presidential form of the governance that state and society attempt to create a point of merger. The continuation of the Governor General's institution in India and Pakistan were evolutionary take offs from the colonial form of statehood, statecraft and polity, even after the departure of British. This is ultimately identical to the separation of state from society, translating itself into the separation between the representatives of the state and that of the people's governance. The institutions of Governor Generals, Presidents and Prime Ministers have bifurcated states and societies into polar opposites. Thus, the establishments of South Asian countries have always kept themselves at bay from their own people and societies. This is the major reason, in terms of political philosophy as well as systems, why societies have expressed their symbolic withdrawal from the state through various social movements.

Invasion of Kashmir, 1948

Kashmir has remained a major cause of disagreement in India-Pakistan relations, which has ultimately had adverse effects on peace and human security in all of South Asia.

Kashmir became a bone of contention when the Pakistan Army, newly craved out of the Royal Indian Army, attacked Kashmir, which according to the settlement of the Indian Partition was a state of India. There are many existing narratives on that particular war of 1948, which have become a centre of debate for historians. However, no historical narratives of the war mention who ordered and authorized the offensive to invade Kashmir. Jinnah, the Governor General and founder of Pakistan, never gave any such orders to the Pakistan Army. It was the then Chief of Army Staff who in fact started the offensive. This breach of political morality and the fundamental norm of the statecraft had long lasting impacts on the politics of Pakistan as well as peace and security in South Asia.

The 1948 Pakistan-India war primarily decided the political future of Pakistan in which the military became the driving force of almost all affairs within and outside the country. Besides, this unauthorized and illegitimate invasion of Kashmir was the core reason behind the six decade-long cold and hot wars between India and Pakistan.

Constitutional illegitimacy

Pakistan was an unexpected and unplanned outcome of the British withdrawal from the subcontinent in 1947. Pakistan had never existed in human history. It was created out of two historically sovereign countries of Sindh and Balochistan and the partition of the Punjab and Pashtun areas from Afghanistan. The country has no politically legitimate constitution since 1947. A couple of constitutions were imposed on the newborn country during1950 - 1970 by military regimes. Moreover, no Constituent Assembly was elected in 1973 to form the constitution.

The break-up of Pakistan in 1971, in which Bangladesh dislodged the so-called two-nation theory of Hindu and Muslim nations and claimed nation-statehood along ethno-linguistic lines, invalidated the foundations on which Pakistan was created. It was therefore imperative, according to international norms and political morality, that the state of Pakistan would have convened a Constituent Assembly through which the four federating states would have reached a new social contract of living within Pakistan. Unfortunately, the military dominated Pakistan and its ethnic Punjabi supremacy did not consider this option. It is therefore that Pakistan today is facing highly popular and massive freedom movements in Sindh and Balochistan.

Unfolding knots

Pakistan is undergoing greater waves of chaos and anarchy due to unreasonable policies, actions and intentions of the security establishment. The dominance of the military in every sphere of the country; the virtual colonization of Sindh, Balochistan and Khyber Pakhtunkhuwa by the Punjabi elite; the unwillingness for a new social contract between the federated provinces after the country's break-up in 1971; and the attachment of the state-ego with Kashmir after an unjustified and unauthorized 1948 Kashmir war are core foundations of Pakistan's rouge state behavior.

Pakistan has to dislodge the many unnecessary strings it has attached through its history. Besides, it has to correct internal political legalities and legitimacies, especially in the context of province-province as well as provinces-federation relations. This essentially requires the separation of religion from the state as well as restricting the role of the military to defense, as devised by the political leadership of the country. These internal and external changes are prerequisites for peace and prosperity within Pakistan and consequently, in the South Asia. Pakistan has to choose one option out of 'decay or destruction.' The time for the third-way is now over.

Published in daily The Kathmandu Post, Nepal on December 24, 2013

DIVIDE & RULE

Don't trap Sindh!

The time has come for Sindhi, especially Sindhi in Diaspora, to seriously opt for taking the formal case of Sindh in the United Nations on the basis of historical treaties signed between sovereign country of Sindh and the Britain before Britain's invasion of Sindh as well as crimes committed by the State of Pakistan and its ethno-communal mercenaries against Sindhi. This has become necessary especially after the recent blackmailing attempts by the sate-cronies.

Blackmailing Sindh

Pakistani establishment has a history of blackmailing the Sindh freedom movement. It usually plays third fiddle in the form of a political group called Mutahida Qaumi Movement (MQM) to counter the rise in the freedom movement in Sindh. This tactics is also used whenever Sindh freedom is discussed in the international circles. This 'Blackmail Sindh' card usually consist the jargons for the division of Sindh on one or the other pretext.

This time this rotten card is used for the multiple purposes that include psychologically pressurizing Sindhi nationalists after the extraordinary rise in the freedom movement, bargaining for the release of General Musharaf since Sindhi people, like previously, are not in the favor of illegal and illegitimate concessions to the retired military dictator and a bid to get more concessions. Besides, it is also an attempt to advance the nefarious racist agenda for the division of Sindh in future.

Unable to divide Sindh

Mutahida Qaumi Movement (MQM) Supremo Altaf Hussain said that either a Chief Minister for Sindh should be an Urdu speaking for every alternate term or Sindh should be divided in the two provinces. Later on, he along with his party's most senior man Anwar Ahmed has demanded new twenty administrative provinces in Pakistan and has quoted the example of India, Iran and Turkey. Let us see briefly the realities behind the issues of new provinces in Pakistan.

An elected member of the provincial assembly, according to the constitution, can be Chief Minister of the province. Majority in the provincial legislature is the only requirement. Unlike its contemporary Pakistan People's Party (having home-ground in Sindh), the MQM is skewed and restricted tightly to the ethno-linguistic Urdu speaking Sindhis.

PPP since last three decades is having our Urdu speaking brothers as the senior most central leaders, ministers, and at least one Deputy Speaker. MQM, however, haven't opened up as yet to even the all people of Sindh. MQM no doubt did an attempt in past to encourage the non-Urdu speakers among its fold; however that attempt was half heartedly since no Sindhi of Sindhi, Baloch and Pashtun origin was taken into the iron clad central fold of the party.

The other options for acquiring the post of the Chief Minister are to lobby with the political parties that have seats in the Sindh Assembly. Unfortunately, MQM has failed to build the rapport with the rest of the Sindh based political parties. On the other hand, the current Governor of Sindh belongs to MQM and has assumed this position of state-power almost twelve years ago despite the fact that newspapers have run several stories about the criminal cases against him. There are many other things that also need to be seen, for example share in civil and military bureaucracy.

Pakistan Army is sixty-seven years old and Sindh Regiment is now forty. Sindhis are bellow one percent in Pakistani armed forces and no Sindhi has been promoted to the post of Brigadier General during the whole history of Pakistan. Meanwhile, dozens of senior and junior Generals have been Urdu speakers including three Army Chiefs. If this clubbed with the Air Force and Naval senior leadership, the revelations would change the very notion that who is deprived in the land of Sindh.

Myth of population behind new provinces

Two, the governance inefficiency and appropriate utilization of resources is a groundless argument for the new administrative provinces. If this argument is seen in the context of federal practices and examples of India, China, UK, USA, Iran and Turkey, such argument would fall in the category of fallacy. India has Uttar Pradesh, the largest federating state among the federations on the globe with the population of 204 million human beings speaking three major languages and dialects. This federating state alone has more population than whole of Pakistan.

China has Guangdong, the second largest populous federating province in the world, with the population of 104 million, more than the total human inhabitation of each Sindh, Balochistan, KP and Punjab. England in UK is the largest federating province among the European federations with the population of 53 million that equals Sindh and is higher than Balochistan and KP.

California in USA is the largest federating state in the northern America with the population of nearly 39 million, slightly thinner than Sindh and thicker than Balochistan and KP. India, China and Iran have mostly old and new states on the ethnic bases as well as a few on the religious-sectarian bases. Turkey has no socio-political and cultural relevance with Pakistan since it is a bi-ethnic country.

These four countries are stable and prosperous nations and are the world powers. This means that governance is a process of efficacy and social justice for the human development, peace and harmony.

Why a province for the recent immigrants is impossible?

No country in the world has yet created a state for the recently migrated communities. This is a kind of disastrous action, which would further create a chaos among the world community. If such an action is taken in the Pakistan, than probably India would be facing the demand for creating a province for Sindhi and Tibetan immigrants, Canada and England would face a demand of province for the immigrants in Vancouver and England.

Besides, if any province is created in any part of the world for the recently migrated / refuge communities, the countries would never open-up their border for the refugees of neighboring or distant countries, in case the some communities flee their homelands due to wars and instability. This would create a new crisis in the world.

What Sindhi should do?

There are many options for Sindhi people to cope with this situation within Pakistan. However, Sindhi people in Sindh and abroad may also consider one important option- legally going in the United Nations against the Federation of Pakistan and United Kingdom on the basis of treaties signed between the sovereign country of Sindh and the Great Britain before 1843 in which British assured security and sovereignty of Sindh from the invasions and other likely threats particularly from Punjab.

British violated their signed treaties in 1947 when its handed over Sindh to the Punjab against the will of Sindhi people. The international legal framework has space for that. Besides, Sindhi in Diaspora should seriously consider on the agenda of the membership of Sindh as an observer state in the United Nations.

Published on www.merinews.com 19 September, 2014

Who Wants to Divide Sindh?

Sindh is on the verge of widespread political violence due to newly announced local government ordinance (in September 2012, which to administratively divide Sindh). The situation can possibly be disastrous for the future political course of Pakistan and might even have disastrous impact on South Asia and the rest of the world.

Sindh is undergoing an unending and nerve taking process of political standoffs since the creation of Pakistan, and therefore, has been continuously struggling since last six decades over the rights, sovereignty, security, and interests of the province and its indigenous underdeveloped majority population.

The issue of Sindhi-Hindu exodus is still waiting to be concluded positively, yet rise of another issue of People's Local Government Act (PLGA) promulgated by the Pakistan People's Party (PPP) and Mutahida Qaumi Movement (MQM) may possibly open a new chapter of popular movement and possibly a slight degree of violence in Sindh. The dilemma of the issue is the violation of citizen's right to information by the government through avoiding to public the text of the ordinance; however some features of the ordinance have been made public by the provincial information minister.

Peopling of the land

Sindh is a demographically vulnerable province. Its indigenous Sindhi-speaking people are almost at the verge of being converted into the permanent minority in their historical land. The linguistic Urdu speaking people who migrated to Pakistan during the partition of united India in 1947 had mostly settled in the urban hubs of the province, which at that time were evacuated by the

Hindus who left Sindh and Pakistan due to fear of violence by these partition-refugees.

The second wave of refugees to Sindh was of ethnic Biharis from Bangladesh who fled the country after supporting Pakistani Army in massacring the ethnic Bengalis. This was followed by the third wave of migration of Pashtuns, which massively began especially after so-called Afghan Jihad against Soviet Union during 1980-90s.

The migration from Punjab was gradual. It came along with every major development initiative, especially during the commissioning of Sukkur, Guddu and Kotri barrages on river Indus, and after development of Sindh Industrial Trading Estates (SITE) near Karachi, Hyderabad, and Sukkur. The other refugees and illegal immigrants in the province are Rohingya Burmese Muslims, Bengalis and various fugitive nationals who came here due to legal loopholes and due to Islamist aspirations of the Pakistan's state policies; thus Sindh has been peopled in the name of Islam as if rest of Pakistan was a non-Muslim territory.

Ethnic and demographic contours

Overwhelming majority in 1947, exclusive native Sindhis are reduced to 65 percent in their province. Urdu-speaking Sindhis (Muhajirs) form 16 to 17 percent and the rest are Pashtuns, Punjabis and others. The demographic features of Karachi are more complex. Those claimed to be 'Muhajirs' by MQM form 40 percent of the city's population, which consists of the decedents of Urdu speaking refugees from pre-partition United Provinces (UP) and Central Provinces (CP) of India, Biharis and Bangalis from Bangladesh, Guajarati Memons who speak variant dialect of Sindhi language, Qaimkhani of Rajasthani dialect and a small number of Mapla Malayalam people. If analyzed on ethno-linguistic basis, exclusively 'Urdu speaking' people form nearly 20-25 percent of the city, according to rough estimates.

If the indigenous people who have settled in the city from rural Sindh during last sixty years combine the indigenous population of the city (decedents of Sindhis of Sindh and Baloch origin residing there before 1947), they will form majority ethnic population of Karachi. The third ethnically significant group is Pashtuns from Balochistan and Khyber Pakhtunkhuwa (KPK).

Governance and development

It is, academically, a well-known fact that civil and military bureaucracy of Pakistan has been predominantly Punjabis and Urdu-speaking refugees since the partition of united India. Therefore, it is not hard to believe that hostility of Pakistan towards India was basically indoctrinated by those who hailed from today's India during the partition in 1947, and took refuge in Pakistan due to fear of violence and better future prospects. They, being a major part of statecraft, also developed their communities within the federation of Pakistan at the cost of others. If seen in the context of Sindh, one may find the worst exploitation in the context of development and in the form of discrimination against the Sindhis. If an honest sociological and ethnographical analysis was carried out, the case of Sindhis in Sindh would be the worst in the federal malpractices and ethnic cleansing on the globe.

There are severe discriminations and development disparities in urban-rural, urban-urban, and urban of the urban and rural of the urban context, which are mostly ethnically biased. The decade long, General Pervez Musharaf's military rule is the worst example of marginalizing, demoralizing, and ethnical devastating of ethnic Sindhis. He carried electoral constituency alterations and engineering in the cities of Sindh in a manner that MQM may win more seats from the areas, where they have even lesser population of supporters.

Politics of ethnically selective options

Karachi comprises five administrative districts before the military government of general Musharraf. During the military regime, the city of nearly 13 million people at that time was converted into one district, and the city government was given similar powers and in some context, more powers than Sindh government. It was a kind of virtual separation of Karachi from the rest of Sindh. On the other hand, Hyderabad city, which had hardly 4 million inhabitants, was divided into four districts. Both these actions were carried out for vote bank politics.

Once this was done, the worst forms of discrimination were carried out when the policies were adopted to deny Sindhi students' admission in higher education institutions of Karachi, whereas Punjabis, Pashtuns, Kashmiris and Gilgit-Baltistanis were allocated a higher number of seats. On the other hand, the century old settlements of Sindhis in Karachi were termed illegal, evacuated and handed over to the land mafia.

Who fears ethnic Sindhis?

Sindhis have a history of non-violence. The only militancy on their part was for the freedom wars of Sindh during British rule in united India. Two elements fear ethnic Sindhis. The security establishment of the country fears their historical pro-democracy and secular role. Besides, exclusively Sindhi populated areas of the province are largest energy houses as well as hub of natural resources of Pakistan, according to the data of Government of Pakistan.

MQM also fears Sindhis due to several reasons, however mainly due to one. There cannot be more influx of linguistically Urdu speaking people in Karachi; whereas the urbanization of Sindhis has now started changing the demographic composition of Karachi, which ultimately means that vote bank and street power of MQM will decrease in upcoming years. MQM claims to be a party of middle class but practically does not seem to be willing to optimizing the vote bank in aftermath of growing urbanization of Sindhis. This ultimately gives a feeling of it being lingual-racial force.

Assumptions of alarming paradox

What can be the worst consequences of the situation? One unfortunate possibility is the violence; whereas the other one is disastrous, which in fact is an assumed scenario.

The politics in Pakistan gives a feeling that there are two lobbies – posing-to be-moderate and advocates of conservatives. MQM is allying with the posing-to be-moderates to further its ethnic agenda through various state and non-state actors in Pakistan, and through engaging international factors that claim to be anti-religious extremism. Paradoxically, Sindhi nationalists, who unlike MQM have been secular throughout the Pakistan history, are at the brink where no posing-to be-liberals from Pakistan and the world support them in protecting and defending the interests of Sindh, its people and their sovereignty in the federation of Pakistan.

It is assumed that in such a possibly grave situation, very limited options are left for Sindhi people, which most probably if opted will leave very meaningful impacts on Pakistan and the liberal world. This is a loud thinking, which may be wrong, if liberal and secular portions of the establishment and concerned world kept on supporting the elements bent on dividing Sindh, then Sindhis possibly feel to have chosen out of two options:

a) Allying with liberals, and secular state and non-state actors. It ultimately means to keep silence on the division of Sindh and becoming Red Indian on their historical land.

b) Associate with the non-liberal, non-democratic, and fundamentalist forces to secure integration of Sindh. If this situation becomes real, then one thinks that the choice is not left for Sindhis. In fact, it is for those whose stakes are in Sindh or in other words, the changing scenario can damage their stakes. If such an assumption becomes close to reality, then upcoming anarchy will be irresistible.

What kind of local governance is required?

Local government is highly important tier of federalism and democracy; however when it is authorized to overlap other tiers, it is the worst form of federalism and democracy. Demographically fragile Sindh requires a local government that at least clearly makes distinction between the local and provincial tier on the following basis so that social harmony, development, and people's issues may be resolved:

a. Local governance should not be authorized to influence and alter the ethnic and demographic complexion of the cities, towns and unions, which means the use and utilization of urban and rural land; regularizing or legitimizing the settlements, community policing that becomes ethnic policing or ethnic parties policing should be under provincial government.

b. Local governance should help the state and its provincial tier but should not have an edge to act as a state in itself. In federalism and democracies, Center and Provinces mostly undertake role of the State at macro management level, whereas local governments mostly manage the micro and non-state nature governance issues. This becomes an imperative when a complex web of social composition and ethnic contest over resources and power is involved. This essentially means the services like police, education, irrigation, coastal management and many others should and must fall under the authority of provincial government.

The integration

The only way forward in the situation is the roadmap of harmony, integration, and inter-dependence between ethnic Sindhi speaking Sindhis and Urdu speaking Sindhis, which unfortunately cannot be attained through any biased and unbalanced local governance system. Let a chance be given to modern nation building in Sindh through harmony and integration. Besides, Pakistan needs to legislate immediately over the inter-provincial migration, right to vote and election contesting.

Published on www.merinews.com September 12, 2012

Ethnicity and Urbanization

The transformation of South Asia from feudal and rural relations into the urban has enormous development contours along with highly sensitive challenges of its ethno-political stability and governance. Therefore, any discourse focusing cities in South Asia cannot avoid the issues and relation between demography, governance, and ethnic stability.

Mega transformation

South Asia amid uncontrolled population growth will have 1.2 billion urban mass by 2050, which no doubt will be the largest urbanization of human history in any single regional entity. It will be a chain-process of transformation, converting a large number of small into big villages, towns into tertiary cities, and existing small cities into the secondary cities. Today's metropolitans will touch their vertical and horizontal heights. The issues of land, population pressure, demography, resources, and governance as well as the niche of harmonized topography and ethnography will be the major focus for the governments.

This process is bound to change the contours of human settlement and development patterns. The change in sociological configuration due to this has already become visible in some countries, where an increasing number of rural and newly born middle class has started attaining power-opportunities in the societies. Secondary cities augment rural development and play the role of sanctuaries of urbanization and help creating new middle class and urban poor; thereby filtering the migrations towards metropolitans.

The situation has further strengthened the fold of broader civil society actors in the region that have started ascertaining their role in the given domains. It is expected that the cities like Delhi, Bangalore, and Lahore will cross their status of second line metropolitans in the upcoming decades. Kathmandu city can also be considered in the queue given the demographic mass and development in Nepal. It is therefore important for the future governance of these cities that the repercussions of uneven development, unplanned urbanization, and fallouts of existing metropolitans should be taken into the consideration.

Ethnicity and conflicts

Population movement has already altered the socio-economic and demographic structure of the cities in the region and will certainly affect it in future. It has already created in some cases deep issues of ethnic conflict, development disparity, and the contest over resource, which also has resulted into violence sometimes. In Asia, such complex example of urbanization based on ethnic diversity and antagonism rooted into the migrations is Jakarta. The other examples are Karachi and to certain extent Bangalore. Karachi is a peculiar case study for the region, where ethno-linguistically non-local migrant minority rules the city in terms of electoral politics as well as use of violence; and legislatively resists the urbanization of native and indigenous Sindhi majority so as their minority rule remain unchallenged.

From the perspective of the growth of urban centers, it is apparent that "net internal migration from rural areas" has played a substantial role in urbanization. According to UN modulated projections, Pakistan's 48.9 percent population will be living in the urban hubs by 2030.

Karachi has a jerky demographic history. Until 1965, it was a Sindhi majority city, in latter two decades it observed a win-win balance between Sindhi-Balochi, Urdu, and Pashtu ethnic groups. Today, it is again Sindhi-cum-Baloch majority city; however politically ethno-linguist Urdu minority of the city rules it. The city has observed around four waves of violence since 1972, which have taken lives of beyond ten thousand citizens.

Governance, demography and discrimination

Six major demographic groups form the politics of ethnic interests in Karachi. Their population-wise sequence would be indigenous Sindhi and Baloch; Urdu and Bihari, Pashtun and Punjabi migrants; indigenous miscellaneous group of naturalized Parsies, Rajasthanis, and illegal migrants and refugees from Afghanistan, Myanmar, Bangladesh and Iran. The peculiar aspect of this ethnic politics is the contest over the resources and opportunities, in which Urdu speaking Muhajir minority rules not only the city but also Sindh province in many ways.

In Karachi, the ethnic minority through ethnically biased governance and legislation is discriminating the development of indigenous people. During the rule of General Musharaf, the electoral constituencies of Sindh were altered in a manner that the indigenous majority may win lesser seats in the provincial and federal legislature.

Recently, the legislation over a controversial and popularly rejected Sindh Local Government Act has stirred up an insurgency like situation. The Act administratively separates Karachi from rest of the province and the Mayor of the city is given more authorities then the Chief Minister of Sindh. It has at least three discriminative aspects. By administratively converting five districts of Karachi into one, it will give edge to ethno-linguistic Urdu speaking minority, which is the absolute majority in only one district, Central Karachi. The Act gives authorities to the Mayor to decree demolishing of a house or a settlement. This has resulted into demolishing of two historical Sindhi Hindus settlements of Karachi within two weeks of its legislation in October 2012. The other ethnic groups of the city fear that this authority would be used against Sindhi, Baloch, Pashtun and Punjabi settlements, which together form nearly 70 percent of the metropolitan.

Lessons for the South Asia

The ongoing urbanization in South Asia is bound to create ethnic diversity in the existing and emerging cities; therefore, if this aspect is not part of urban planning, the ethnic chaos is inevitable. Avoiding urban conflicts, the right to rule and opportunities needs to be ensured to the ethnic indigenous population.

The urbanization in South Asia will also be carrying along the issues like poor governance, limited resources, housing, non-futuristic planning; infrastructure inadequacy; transportation lethargy and environmental problems. This requires adopting modern frameworks of urban planning, comprehensive master plans, efficient land-use, and appropriate zone regularization as well as building control. The future of South Asian cities could only be save through non-traditional and futuristic vision and planning that does not compromise rights of the land, native population as well as city dwellers.

Published in daily The Kathmandu Post, Nepal on November 27, 2013

Political and ethnic battles turn Karachi into Beirut of South Asia

In Pakistan, powerful ethnic minorities rule the under-developed majorities. In the context of Sindh, especially in Karachi, this ethnic contest of power has turned this historical land into Beirut of South Asia.

Sindh is a volcano of ethnic frictions. The simmering violence in its capital Karachi during last ten years has taken 5549 lives, whereas 227 lost lives during first eight months of 2012. It can potentially explode into the higher scale conflicts, if authorities in the twin cities of Islamabad-Rawalpindi do not address it appropriately.

The conflict profile of Sindh and its capital Karachi is highly peculiar case study of South Asia. Like many other conflicts of the region, it contains partition legacy as well as ethnic contest for power and recourses, which are foundations of the antagonism. It has many peculiarities also. The important feature of the situation is the dominating recently migrated ethnic minority versus underdeveloped majority indigenous people.

Miniature of migrations

The migrations from divided India to Pakistan in 1947, and followed by the mass migrations from Bangladesh due to the partition of Pakistan in 1971 is a widely discussed background of the ethnic conflict in Sindh. The province is peopled by the human flows after 1947 from the Indian provinces which are today called Uttar Pradesh, Delhi, Andhra Pradesh, Gujarat, Rajasthan and Maharashtra; later on in 1971 and thereafter from Dhaka, Rajishri, Rangpur, Khulna and Chittagong divisions of Bangladesh; and finally after 1980s from Afghanistan, Burma and rest of the Pakistani provinces.

If analyzed, there are two indigenous ethno-linguistic groups in Sindh -- Sindhis forming majority by being 65 percent of the province, Baloch of Makrani and Jadgali (Sindhi) origin mostly settled in Karachi, and the third one is semi-indigenous Sindhi ethnic groups of Memons and Kutchis who migrated from Kutch and Bhuj - the Sindhi areas of Indian Gujarat.

The post-1947 mass migrations have three categories: Indian partition refugees, whose second and third generation is inhibiting Sindh; 1971 war refugees whose first and second generation is inhibiting the province, and finally post-1980 refugees, who either illegally migrated to Sindh or sought refuge due to Afghan war and Burmese crises.

Who is who of ethnicities in Sindh?

The strings of politics in Sindh, especially in its capital Karachi can only be understood through ethno-linguistic point of view. Nine ethno-linguistic groups are residing Sindh particularly in Karachi. It would be wise to understand their characteristics.

- *Indigenous Sindhis:* Indigenous population of Samat and Baloch origin that speak, read, and write in Sindhi language and claim Sindhi identity.

- *Indigenous Baloch:* People of Makrani coastal Baloch background who speak Balochi and claim Balochi identity; however can understand and talk Sindhi language due to being indigenous inhabitants of Karachi.

- *Indigenous Sindhi of Gujarati and Lasi origin:* There are two groups in this category. Speakers of Memoni and Kutchis dialects of Sindhi language migrated to Karachi from Sindhi areas of Kutch and Bhuj of Gujarat, India and settled in Karachi before and after 1947. Whereas Lasi are ethno-linguistically Sindhi who hailed from Lasbela princely state of Sindhi population, administratively annexed to Balochistan during 1960s.

- *Rajasthanis:* Mostly consist three Muslim clans of Qaimkhani Rajputs, Silawats, Gazdars and Shaikhs. Majority of them speak various dialects of Rajasthani language; however can understand and speak Sindhi. Silawats migrated to Sindh during 1930s on the invitation by Pir Pagaro. Gazdar came even earlier. Later both are also considered as an indigenous population; meanwhile earlier two clans are culturally and linguistically similar to Sindhis.

- *Malayalam Maplas*: Migrated from Kerala province of India to Sindh in 1935 after Maplapuram movement in Kerala during British Raj. They identify themselves as Mapla or Malabari.

- *Urdu speakers/ Muhajirs:* Speak Lukhnavi and Khariboli dialects of Urdu language and migrated after 1947 mostly from Delhi, Uttar Pradesh and Andhra Pradesh provinces of today's India. They identify themselves as Urdu speakers or Muhajir.

- *Bihari:* Bhojpuri lingual community migrated from Bangladesh after 1971 that identifies itself as Bihari.

- *Punjabi:* Migrated from Pakistani Punjab province before and after 1947 in search of employment; after commissioning of barrages in Sindh especially when hundreds of Punjabi landless peasants were given thousands of acres land in Sindh during 1950 – 1971; and after installation of many cantonments in the various cities of Sindh.

- *Pashtun:* Migrated after military rule of Pakhtunkhuwa generals Ayub Khan and Yahya Khan. A large number of them migrated from Afghanistan after the Afghan Jihad against Soviet Union in post 1980s.

- *Bengalis:* Those who did not either go to Bangladesh after 1971 or migrated to Sindh from there illegally after 1990s.

- The rest are a small number of mix population of Maharashtrans, Burmese, Goans, Siraikis, Hindkos and Kashmiris.

If first three categories of indigenous population were combined, the indigenous majority population would roughly count beyond 68 percent. If the Indian partition Muhajirs/ Urdu speakers and Bangladeshi refugees of Bengali and Bihari origin are combined, they will roughly form bellow 19 percent of the province. In Karachi, if the indigenous population is combined, they will form roughly beyond 40 percent. If exclusively Urdu speaking and Bihari / Bhojpuri speaking are combined, they will count bellow 25 percent of the city. If Sindhi speaking of Samat and Baloch origin are counted (excluding Makrani Balochs and Guajarati Memons) they will cross 30 percent in the city. If map of Karachi is analyzed the Urdu and Bihari speaking majority absolutes districts will form bellow 10 percent of city's geography.

An undisclosed demography

Sindh has 23 administrative districts out of which five form Karachi city. If these are ethnically analyzed on the principles of absolute majority, simple majority, and mix population based on the 1998 census and last 15 years migration trend, an entirely new scenario will come out.

In the category of absolute majority, Sindhis are an absolute majority in 17 districts including district Malir of Karachi, whereas Muhajirs/ Urdu speakers dominate one district of Karachi Central. Sindhis are in simple majority in Karachi East as well as Hyderabad district. If culturally similar ethnic groups are clubbed, Sindhis and Baloch are absolute majority in district South Karachi followed by Punjabis as well as Burmese and Bengalis illegal immigrants. Muhajirs / Urdu speakers and Biharis, if combined, are majority in District West Karachi followed by Balochis, Pashtuns and Sindhis. Sindhis and Balochis dwell in strategically lesser important areas, mostly out of extremely central orbit of the city, and a large number is rural population of the Karachi, which is divided in several electoral constituencies. This gives an edge to MQM, with a highly organized mechanism and use of violence, to hold the city even representing a minority ethnic group.

One in the same thing: urban and rural feudalism

The fundamental meaning of term 'feudal lord' is the one who hold power of war making and feud management in certain rural geography. Mode of production has been their source of keeping private armies, which in classical terms remains agriculture and pastoral.

The power in Sindh lies in two hands: feudal of rural Sindh, which is mostly Sindhi and urban-feudal of Karachi city, which is mostly Urdu speaker; however, in Hyderabad both are the Urban feudal. Rural feudal in Sindh are feudal in material terms having Sindhi variant of mercenaries and exploiting peasantry, whereas urban feudal have characteristic of classical feudal lords, which means keeping urban mercenaries for the feuds and violence to exploit urban poor and to take hold of majority ethnic groups of the city.

Both behave almost similarly except that the earlier behave in rural and unorganized manner and later behave in urban and well-organized way. There are paradoxical behaviors in both. One can oppose and contest a rural feudal in Sindh and not necessarily be killed due to this action; however such action necessarily invite a murder attempt by the urban lords. Rural feudal are secular unlike their urban counterparts. Urban feudal meanwhile behave positively regarding the matters like infrastructure development, in which their rural counterparts are parasites.

PPP, MQM, and Sindhi nationalists

A large number of Sindhi feudal lords and a small number of Urdu speaking and Sindhi middle class normally control Pakistan People's Party (PPP) in Sindh. Ethno-linguist Urdu speaking Muhajir people usually control MQM. Mostly Sindhi nationalists and PPP – Murteza Bhutto group, a splinter group of PPP, oppose PPP in Sindh. Two groups oppose MQM openly -- MQM splinter group led by Aafaq Ahmed, and the Bihari population of Karachi. Ethnic Biharis in Karachi, after the murder of second most popular leader of MQM Imran Farooq in London, formed Bihari Qaumi Movement (BQM) in Karachi. Sindhi politicians are also divided into ideological groups: secessionists, advocates of provincial autonomy, and federalists.

PPP and MQM have a few basic common interests therefore they tend to ally. Both want to keep their vote bank and hegemony intact in their area of support (rather control). Both mostly do not challenge each other in the election contest except a few constituencies in Karachi and Hyderabad; therefore, they consider themselves natural allies. MQM's street control of Karachi is also important factor. It has a history that whenever a government, no matter they are part of it or opposition, denies or delays their demands, Karachi observe violence. It is the fear of violence in the economic capital of Karachi that they are becoming coalition partners in various governments since last 15 years.

Basis of contemporary conflict

The basis of ongoing contest and conflict in Sindh are a few but highly important:

- Contest on the distribution of resources combined by development not on the urban-rural bases alone, but on the ethnic bases as well. This includes urban-rural and district-district disparities at

Karachi city level, urban-urban at provincial level, which means between the cities where either ethnicity is in the significant number and between urban- rural in general across the province.

- Growing urbanization has started changing the demographic characteristic and population size of the cities across the Pakistan especially in Sindh province. In Sindh, this ultimately means the change in the ethnic composition of the cities, which are ethnically diverse. An overwhelming majority of non-Punjabi refugees, who migrated from India after partition of sub-continent, settled in the cities of Sindh. Therefore, urbanization in Sindh today means urbanization of Sindhis. MQM, which has been containing electoral rule in Karachi and Hyderabad even having typically Urdu speaking minority in both of the cities, has fear of losing hold of cities in terms of electoral and street power.

- MQM wants a political edge of ethnic aspects in provincial and local government system. The admissions of Sindhi students are already banned in Karachi educational institutions; and now the one who have not been born in Karachi cannot get a government job there. MQM wants some important departments under the local government's control that include police, revenue, land utilization, colonization and settlements, education and fisheries along with others. This ultimately gives feeling to Sindhi population of virtual separation of Karachi from Sindh and resisting their right to urbanization and development in their historical land. Sindhi nationalists have apprehensions regarding MQM politics that have grown since the military rule of General Pervez Musharraf. The general altered the constituencies of Karachi and Hyderabad city in a manner that Sindhi voters may not influence majority of the seats, meanwhile MQM may win from the areas where it has not majority ethnic support. Besides, indigenous Sindhi think that an organized minority, which is virtually ruling the province since 1947, keep aspirations of carving out a separate province out of Sindh. This of their feeling was further strengthened when MQM presented a bill in the national assembly in 2011 for creating new provinces in Pakistan, which mentioned in its preamble that provinces are not sacred and can be divided.

The nature of recently promulgated Sindh People Local Governance Ordinance / Act (SPLGA) has infuriated Sindhi nationalists enough that they gave a call of strike on September 13, which was successful without the use of violence. In Karachi two districts – East and Malir - out of five were on complete strike, meanwhile district South observed partial strike; however, majority areas of district Central and West remained open.

Local governance system

SPLGA gives a feeling that Sindh has become an independent country and it transfers some of its authorities to the autonomous district/ city governments. It is virtual attempt to divide Sindh into five autonomous divisions; more authorized then practices within the federations around the globe in terms of political systems. According to a Karachi based analyst, it transfers various state authorities of the provincial tier to the Municipals and Districts led by a Mayors and Chairpersons. The authorities include land use and utilization, revenue, housing and settlement authorities and even recruitment of provincial departments in the districts.

Sovereignty of provincial government is compromised in a manner that a degree of autonomy is given to the districts beyond the provincial supremacy. According to the ordinance, as analyzed by a Karachi based journalist, if a proposed scheme or plan by a district / divisional government to the provincial government is not accepted or ratified by the later within sixty days, it would legally become approved. Besides preparation of master plans, local governments are also transferred the authority to approve zoning, classification, and reclassification of land, environment control, urban design, urban renewal, and ecological balances. Their approval authorities are vested in the Municipal / District Councils. It also transfer the authorities to review implementation of rules and bye-laws governing land use, housing, markets, zoning, environment, roads, traffic, tax, infrastructure and public utilities. Besides, the 'properties' and all concerned matters are handed over to the district and municipal tiers.

Primarily it hands over various departments of the provincial nature to the districts. It also authorizes the district government to change the quantity of officials and size of these departments; recruit employees directly and enhance ten percent budget for additional recruitments. Such authorities, according to a Karachi-based journalist, were also given in the Musharaf's local government ordinance, which gave edge to MQM recruiting forty thousand new employees. Almost all of them did not only belong to single ethnicity of the city, but also were the cadres and activists of MQM. Political parties has been alleging since last many years that the violence is Karachi has been carried thereafter through these cadres by using city government machinery.

Union Councilor (neighborhood representative), in the ordinance, are authorized to recruit the security guards directly. This ultimately has enhanced apprehensions that if a party having militant capacity wins local government elections, it can recruit its cadres as guards and keep on dominating people through the legitimized use of violence.

The ordinance also maintains supremacy of municipal/ district government over Tehsil / sub-district and union level. This will give an edge of ethnic dominancy in the districts of Karachi, which do not contain absolute majority of any single ethnicity. Two districts of Karachi – Central and West – have an overwhelming majority of ethnic Urdu speaking and Bihari people jointly, but there are at least two towns / sub-districts there, which are having Sindhi, Baloch and Pashtun majority population. In such cases, supremacy regarding recourses allocation at district level can discriminate them. The similar issues may occur in the district East, Malir and South as well, which are mostly Sindh-Baloch-Pashtun majority districts. SPLGA gives a feeling that it is a district-states / city-states ordinance, which essentially contradicts the principles of the federation.

What is the way forward?

A set of comprehensive steps is required in the province to foster harmony and interdependency between various ethnic groups meanwhile maintaining ultimate rights of both.

- In presence of Sindh (legislative) Assembly, the ordinance enforced by the Governor is similar to the British rule practices. This ordinance should be taken back; instead, a bill for local government should be tabled in the house for the legislation after undergoing a vast consultation with political parties, representatives of the ethnic groups, civil society, and experts.

- No local government law should supersede the sovereign and autonomous authority of the provincial government, which means the departments, subjects, fields and matters that are of highly provincial nature must not be handed over to the district or municipal governments in an autonomous manner.

- Land use, utilization, revenue, recruitments, approval of schemes and plans and determining the size of departments are the issues that has been used for ethnic dominancy and discrimination. They have also been utilized for changing electoral and ethnic compositions of towns, constituencies, and districts. Therefore, they should be under the provincial authority.

- A plan for a weapon free Karachi should be devised. Until all violence-making forces are not made armless, the peace cannot be ensured in the city.

- Sindhi is official language of the province and a mandatory subject for non-Sindhi speaking population in the primary education; but the practice is otherwise. Ethnic harmony will be unachievable until this is not being done.

- Enforcing agenda of less than 20 percent population over Sindh and of lesser than 25 percent population of Karachi over the city will create an unending anarchy over the upcoming decades. The day people realized that federation is not willing to undone this process, they will popularly bid farewell to the federation.

- If there can be Afro and Asian Americans or Europeans, there can be Sindhi speaking Sindhis, Urdu-speaking Sindhis, Bihari-speaking Sindhis and Pashto-speaking Sindhis and Punjabi-speaking Sindhis. This requires their integration with ethnic Sindhi population and loyalty to the interests of the province.

- Pakistan is a federation of historical sovereign counties of pre-British occupation; therefore a necessary legislation should be made over the inter-provincial migrations, their right to vote in Sindh, contest elections, and holding of public offices. This is the time when indigenous populations' right to rule in their historical homelands needs to be ensured in Pakistan.

- Both MQM and Sindhi nationalists should accept and adopt the term of 'Urdu speaking Sindhis' rather than Muhajirs, which gives no sense that which Muhajirs (refugees) are being pointed out as in last 65 years there have been many waves of different ethno-linguist refugees and migrants towards Sindh.

- If the federation is not able to protect sovereignty of Sindh and its majority indigenous population, and then Sindhi people will be justified to reclaim that sovereignty beyond the federation.

Published on www.merinews.com on September 24, 2012

HUMAN RIGHTS & CIVIL LIBERTIES

Plight of Hindus in Pakistan

The pseudo Muslims, ignorant of the real spirit of Islam, recently exhumed and humiliated the mortal remains of one Bhuro Bhil, a Dravidian Hindu, in district Badin of Sindh province. The land, where he was buried, was in fact donated to the village residents by his ancestors.

As expected, almost all political and social corners of Sindhi society condemned and massively protested against this act of barbarianism. A clear massage has tweeted across the country and the region that there is no space for religious extremism in the secular Sindh. Bilawal Bhutto of Pakistan People Party asked Sindh Government to take actions against the culprits.

The Hindu and Muslim activists from Hindu majority districts of Mithi and Umerkot said that Hindus and Muslims of Sindh are in harmony and both follow the same saint Jhooley Lal. A Hindu temple and a Muslim mosque is under one roof at the shrine of Jhulelal near the Hyderabad city. Meanwhile, Sindhi nationalists have vociferously said that the Mullahs involved in the act were supported by the 'omnipowerful' of Pakistan.

Sindhi Hindus are continuously being victimized since 1948 - earlier at the hands of migrated Muslims from Northern India and now by the state-sponsored Mullahs. Thousands of them have bid farewell to Sindh, Pakistan so far since the Movement for Restoration of Democracy (MRD) during the military regime of General Zia in 1980s. At least, roughly speaking, beyond one hundred thousand Hindus have left the country in last three decades due to persecution mostly unleashed after the establishment of Pano Aqil Cantonment, the largest military installation within Pakistan.

A rim of zealot Madaris (seminaries) were established in Sindh in 1990s and 2000s mostly near Pano Aqil as well as near Indian bordering Thar Desert, where majority of Mullahs are being imported from Punjab and to some extent from Pakhtunkhuwa provinces. These Madaris are, no doubt, the epicenter of harassing and terrorizing Hindus in Sindh who still count 8.5 million in the province.

The people of Sindh have been massively protesting against such kind of barbarism. What needs to be done to address these issues? The 'to do list' is very simple and doable, if the intention of the Pakistan government and security regime are fair.

Before general Zia's martial law, the Sindh Textbook Board's designed curriculum included not only the poetry of some Hindu poets, but also some lessons on the Sindhi Hindus and Parsis who have remained icons of humanity for their services to the poor of Subcontinent particularly in Sindh, Gujarat, Punjab and Maharashtra (provinces in pre-1947 partition of united India). Such characters were Sami, Diya Ram Gidumal, Jamshed Nasarwanji Mehta, Herananad, Kishanchand Bewas and others.

The military regime of Gen Zia ordered the exclusion of these lessons from the textbooks in Sindh. It is a need of the hour that the textbooks for the schools in Sindh should re-include those lessons and poetry (Some poems are still part of the primary level textbooks in Sindhi).

Certain Madaris particularly some those situated in Ghotki, Shikarpur, Sukkur, Khairpur and Umerkot districts have been given a "heavenly" task of forcibly converting Hindus particularly Hindu girls to Islam. The notorious extremist Mullahs and their cronies, commanded by their masters, have been playing with the life, honor, will, and individual liberty of Sindhi Hindu girls in the name of Islam.

The dacoits and looters in the northern Sindh get weaponry from the networks that exist in northeastern Pakistan especially associated with Pakistan's Wah Ordnance Factory. These armed rackets mostly run by the retired army men should be disbanded.

The police and law enforcing agencies should also stop the patronage of the dacoits because in many cases these are used in kidnapping Hindus.

Pakistan Evacuee Trust law categorizes the left over property of Hindus as 'enemy property'. Such a phrase in the law should be deleted because the language of law indicates that the Hindu are considered enemy by the state of Pakistan.

Land has also been a major reason behind some of the minority harassment and victimization incidents in Sindh as well as in rest of the Pakistan. Therefore, land mafias and their supporters should be brought to the books. There should also be devised a code of conduct for purchasing land from communities to construct new human settlements in the cities.

A judicial commission should be formed at the Sindh High Court and Pakistan Supreme level to examine the issues if Hindus and Christian flee their homeland due to failure of governance in providing Hindus security and the safety.

Provincial governments should form special cells to focus the issues of minorities and provide them maximum civil administrative and legal support.

Sindhi Hindus, despite leaving Sindh, should form their Scouts to ensure their community protection and Sindh Government should facilitate them with providing arms and ammunition licensees for the community policing.

Besides, the political parties including nationalists should form district, tehsil, and town level committees focused on the supporting and protecting Hindus. If government fails to provide appropriate safety to Hindus, let the people come out and teach the tough lessons to these sponsored Mullahs who serve the duty of evil in the name of Islam.

If the suggested measures are adopted by the other federating states in Pakistan for the protection of Christian, Hindu, and Sikh there, the life and situation of religious minorities in Pakistan may become changed.

Weather these suggestions would suit the vague internal security doctrine of Pakistan? Incomprehensible! The only thing that is very well known to the people of Sindh that humanity, democracy, and Islam bounds majorities to protect minorities in their territories.

Published on _www.merinews.com_ *13 December, 2013*

No room for Dissent in Pakistan

It was an end of the beginning. Idle to the unforeseen world-shaking incidents like 9/11, Khakis chose military takeover of Pakistan in 1999 pushing the country into a non-democratic mode of government. Eventually, due to gross human rights violations, the anger simmered-up taking citizenry and lawyers to the streets.

It was the first law of motion in the political physics of Pakistan that the military regimes and civil rights were equally opposite. A new chapter of gross human rights violations that Pakistan saw during last military rule has no full stop even today.

Abduction of the dissent

The involuntary disappearances and abductions by the security outfits in Pakistan have been dominating the human rights violations scene since the last decade. If seen in the state-society relations, this had a two-pronged dynamics.

One, the state suppressed political dissent by choosing militarization over the dialogue particularly against Sindhi and Baloch ethnic-nationalists. Two, the state attempted to quarantine some religious non-state elements with which it earlier partnered in the strategic warring in the name of Jihad against Soviet Union and India in Afghanistan and India held Kashmir respectively. The latter provided an excuse to Pakistan to justify earlier actions with the concerned international community. It led to hundreds of reported as well unreported cases of arbitrary disappearances and confinements. According to the Commission of Inquiry on Enforced Disappearances, it has received around 861 new cases of disappearances during January 2011- February 2013 mostly of political dissenters from Balochistan and Sindh provinces.

In 2012, Peshawar High Court ordered investigations into over 100 dead bodies found with marks of tortures across the Peshawar city. On April 21, 2011, security officials according to Human Rights Commission of Pakistan (HRCP) fact-finding report burned three ethnic-Sindhi political leaders alive because they were advocating the right to self-determination for Sindh. On May 22, 2012, Muzaffar Bhutto a prominent leader of an ethnic-Sindhi party was found dead on a roadside in Hyderabad city of Sindh province.

Security officials, according his family and human rights bodies, abducted him in 2011, which was also complained with Office of Commissioner of Human Rights (OCHR) at the United Nations, Geneva. This was followed by the alleged poisoning of Bashir Qureshi, a popular ethnic Sindhi nationalist leader, who died in mysterious circumstances on April 7, 2012 after his party took hundreds of thousands of Sindhis to the streets of Karachi on March 23, 2012 demanding independence.

Blasphemizing Pakistan

Dozens were booked in the notorious blasphemy law in 2012, along with the detention of a 14-year old minor girl Rimsha suffering from Down's syndrome. Meanwhile, 16 others remained on the death row. The harassment and fear created due to the blasphemy epiphany forced Christians in Islamabad, Lahore, Faisalabad, and some other cities of Pakistani Punjab to flee their settlements. In fact, the recent phenomenon of creating fearful environment and torching the Christian and Ahmadi Muslim settlements has its roots in the land mafia and mullah nexus.

Most of the non-Muslim settlements in Punjab are suburban, therefore attractive to the civil and military land entrepreneurs yearning for the urban land in central Punjab cities, which has a higher rate of expansion than rest of Pakistan. Therefore, it would not be wrong to say that the civil and military land grabbers have invisible connections in the recent blasphemy cases in Pakistan along with the agenda of far-right wing within the establishment.

Some research studies mention that the Pakistani police have registered around 4,000 blasphemy cases since 1986. Religious terrorists gunned down at least 20 of them during last decade. If analyzed on the lines of demography in the power matrix, most of the blasphemy cases were registered in seven districts of central Punjab that house 81 percent of Pakistani Christians. Besides, majority of the civil and military bureaucracy of the country hails from these seven districts, which include Lahore, Faisalabad, Sialkot, Kasur, Sheikhupura, Gujranwala, and Toba Tek Singh.

A higher economic contest is found there between civil and military elite and middle class particularly in terms of land utilization and entrepreneur. In fact, these districts are (dis)credited for being an epicenter of Blasphemizing and Talbanizing the rest of Pakistan. Besides, the extremist right wing in Pakistan indents wooing the West and India through harassing minorities because they simply think that Christians and Hindus are demographic allies of the West and India.

According to 1998 Census, minorities count for 3.7 percent out of which Hindus were 1.9 percent. However, the real percentage of Hindus in Pakistan is just beyond 6 percent. Today, 98 percent of Pakistani Hindus live in Sindh with the population of nearly 8 million. The growing Talibanization of Sindh province has caused continuous victimization and persecution of Hindus especially through kidnapping their girls and their reported forced conversion. This has caused gradual exodus of Hindus from Pakistan mostly towards India. According some data, around 5000 Hindus from Sindh reside in the refugee camps in Rajasthan. Their number in Delhi is also significant.

The Hindu exodus from Pakistan has three major political and economic reasons. Primarily, their exodus will create a space for Punjabis and Pashtun refugees from Taliban-insurgency tribal areas to be settled there; meanwhile the Punjabi entrepreneur and trader is eying to replace the fleeing Hindu who is the backbone of rural as well as second line cities economy in Sindh. Besides, it will also serve the demographic and security interests of the omnipresent security establishment, which is converting Sindhis into demographic minority in their own historical land. In addition, it will eventually lead towards Talibanization of Sindh, which is as of now the only secular province of Pakistan.

Another human rights violation has astonished the people of Pakistan that unlike for Ahmadiya Muslims, 2012 was a highly disastrous for Shia Muslims whose 325 persons were targeted and killed, majority of whom were ethnic Hazara from Balochistan.

Freedom of expression

The phenomenal increase in the murder of Pakistani journalists is because independent journalism obstructs the interests of trigger-happy security regime. According to Committee to Protect Journalists (CPJ), Pakistan has become a security-concerned zone after 9/11, where 140 political activists, journalists, academicians, and students were killed in extrajudicial killings since 2010. At least eight journalists were killed in Pakistan during ongoing year, including six in the month of May alone.

In the line of violence

Violence in Pakistan has created anarchy like situation with various connotations of ethnically counter-militancy against the indigenous Sindhi and Baloch people; the terror by religious extremists; and finally the targeted murders due to political antagonism. According to the HRCP reports for 2010, as many as 12,580 people were murdered and over 17000 cases of abduction were reported along with 338 murders by law enforcing agencies in encounters and recovery of at least 174 persons from their illegal detention. According to the Citizens Police Liaison Committee 2,032 ethno-politically motivated targeted killings and 1,790 incidents of kidnappings have been reported in Karachi. Analysts have documented that 2013 through 2011, around 5,549 were killed in the city. In 2013, according to Human Rights Commission of Pakistan (HRCP) 1726 were killed in the first six months in Karachi city alone. Besides, around 356 lost lives during the military operations in the various parts of Pakistan. Meanwhile, 241 dead bodies of tortured activists were recovered from Sindh and Balochistan.

Humanizing the power ethos

Pakistan is feared to slip into the irrecoverable anarchy if it does not adopt humane procedures and practices for military engagement besides reining in the non-state actors involved in the human rights violations. These violations are considered as crime according to the various international treaties, instruments, and bodies under United Nations. Pakistan requires a human rights audit to prevent maxim human persecutions and assassinations.

Published on www.merinews.com 17 July, 2013

Talbanisation of Pakistan

& plight of Christians and Ahmadiya Muslims

Pakistan seems to be on the brink of religious anarchy. Talbanization of the country has turned Punjab province into a hell for the Christian and Ahmadiya religious minorities. Does country intend to adopt the path of harmony? Silence is the only answer!

On the pretext of blasphemy, around two hundred houses of innocent Christians were set on fire a couple of weeks ago by a fanatic mob led by extremist organizations in Lahore, the capital of Punjab province of Pakistan. This has recently been followed by insurrecting Ahmadiya Muslim minority's houses in the province. Violence against religious minorities has been on the increase in the most populous province of the country.

Fear and fury has gripped Pakistani Christians and Ahmadiya Muslims; some of them have fled the province while others are considering fleeing Pakistan. The issue has raised the concerns of international community, particularly the western governments.

The shadow of continuous Hindu exodus has already created fury in Sindh province. Blazing a couple hundred houses of Christians has not only jolted the country, emotionally, but has also pointed towards insensitivity of liberal middle class towards minorities. In fact, the eastern-Indus Pakistan has lurched in the psychological chaos. Needless to mention, the western-Indus is already undergoing Taliban and Baloch freedom movements.

The harassment of minorities in Punjab province has a weird history and sociopolitical context. Punjab, today, has three out of five living rivers from which it gained its name, but the statecraft after the partition of Indian subcontinent in 1947 has created five Punjabis within the Punjabi people -- the Punjab of Taliban;

Christians and Ahmadiya minorities; liberal middle and urban elites; the maneuvered to be non-toleration poor masses and the omnipresent military. Each one is exclusively different from the others, has conflicts of class, culture, cast and ideology but at the same time they share common socio-economic interests.

Wars always have an ugly fall. Their backlash is a plague. Punjab and rest of Pakistan is suffering from the backlash of wars - the cold and hot wars, the proxy and cozy wars - launched by the establishment consisting of migrated Punjabis and Urdu speaking majority. Today, the common Punjabi along with the others in Pakistan is harvesting the crime, which they never sowed. Their only sin was the sycophancy for the criminals, who preferred to be mercenaries of Jihad than that of becoming kings of cultural ethos of Indus civilization.

The divided Punjabi society is at odds with each other. Exporting Taliban to Pashtun, Baloch and Sindhi societies has infected Punjab so much that the term 'Punjabi Taliban' was tossed a couple of years ago by Pakistani politicians and media. This has increased the intolerance in whole Pakistan and flooded hatred in Punjab, not only in the form of victimizing minorities, but also harassing women and children. The number of honor killings, rape cases, and acid attacks taking place there in a year is higher than that of Sindh, Balochistan and Khyber Pakhtunkhwa provinces.

There is another factor too, which needs to be focused. The Jihadi missionary, thousands of Madrasas and religio-cultural influence of conservatives have changed the cultural fabric of Punjab to a greater extent and of the other provinces to some extent. The missionaries in Pakistan are converting those who are already Muslims since centuries from Sunni *Hanfiya* or Shia *Jafferi* sects of Islam to the Salafism or Devband – both in Pakistan have radical background. Why should anyone be allowed to use Pakistani or Afghanistan soil for the Arab nationalist war under the cover of radical Islam against the West in the name of Jihad?

When it comes to Punjab the liberal urban elite keep silent. Salman Taseer, the slain Governor of Punjab, was the only one who spoke boldly and was killed; but this politically less-entity Punjabi middle class remained practically unmoved. A handful of civil society alone protested in the province. It was not due to fear of life alone; it was due to fear of revolting against the Punjabi dominated civil and security establishment, the intolerant and fanatic large number of the population in the province and against those who were not only created from their land, but also fought everywhere in their "broader interests".

In this situation, minorities in Pakistan especially Christians in Punjab province are hopeless. Hindus in Sindh are lucky that Sindh is defending its secular credentials, but for how long the marginalized and oppressed Sindhi people will keep on being Don Quixote.

Talbanization in Pakistan should not be taken for the engagement of Taliban on the western fronts. It has new meanings, which wear many social connotations. It is the Talbanization of Pakistani society and the state apparatus, especially of Punjab, which has culminated into the militancy at Afghan borders.

The plate of Pakistan is not empty yet. In Udero Lal town near Hyderabad of Sindh, Hindu Temple and a Mosque are under one roof near the saint Jhooley Lal, where common Sindhis from both of the beliefs mostly visit, pay homage and perform their religious prayers. Let the sanity come out of an exceptional village of Sahiwal district in Punjab where Muslims and Christians share same graveyard, and when Milad and Christmas coincided in 2009, the joint celebrations were carried out.

It is Punjab and its middle class essentially who needs to emerge against this in association with the other ethnicities. They need to re-federate Pakistan on the new lines of equality, liberalizing state and materialize judicious share of power and resources between federating provinces besides securing and developing minorities.

It is highly important to legislate for the protection of minorities, and repealing laws that can victimize them; however, it is more important to undergo the process of liberalizing, if not secularizing Pakistan society. This is the only way out. All other roads lead to the worst forms of anarchy.

Published on www.merinews.com on 27 March, 2013

Crimes against Humanity in Sindh and Pakistan

Pakistani Foreign Minister Hina Rabani Khar has presented a rosy human rights report in the periodical human rights review session of the United Nations in Geneva held in November 2012, which was an attempt to hide underway crimes against humanity in the country.

She claimed remarkable achievements regarding rights regime in Pakistan. Her report and talk at Geneva gives an impression that Pakistan has undergone a huge transformation during last four years similar to a revolution in the governance, rights regime, and legal framework.

The realities in Pakistan are entirely opposite to that report. If an analysis of last four years in Sindh province alone is carried regarding the Hindus exodus and ethnic cleansing, involuntarily disappearances, extra-judicial killings, and ethnically discriminative legislations, the intensity of the violations as well as denial of the rights under various treaties and declarations of United Nations will no doubt prove to be the crime against humanity.

Hindu Exodus and other forms of ethnic cleansing in Sindh

Thousands of Sindhi Hindus have been forced to quit Sindh, Pakistan, who have refuge or settled in the various countries mostly in India. Nearly 8000 Hindus from Sanghar district of Sindh, Pakistan have sought asylum in Rajasthan state of India during October 2012. The other form of ethnic cleansing is the target killings of ethnic Sindhi, Baloch, and Pashtun in Karachi city, which is aimed to resist these peoples settlement and force the existing population to migrate from city. The state support to a Karachi based ethnic violence-making group through administrative decisions and legislative initiatives is an established reality of violating the various international treaties and declarations, which are rectified by Pakistan.

In this regards, the Convention on the Prevention and Punishment of the Crime of Genocide in Article II reads:

> "....genocide means any of the following acts committed with intent to destroy, in whole or in part, a national, ethnical, racial or religious group, as such: a. killing members of the group; b. causing serious bodily or mental harm to members of the group; c. deliberately inflicting on the group conditions of life calculated to bring about its physical destruction in whole or in part..."

According to the Article III of the convention, genocide; conspiracy to commit genocide; direct and public incitement to commit genocide; attempt to commit genocide; and complicity in genocide are punishable crimes. The article IV of the treaty clearly mentions, "Persons committing genocide or any of the other acts enumerated in article III shall be punished, whether they are constitutionally responsible rulers, public officials or private individuals."

Pakistan, being a signatory of the convention, is bound to amend the constitution in accordance with this convention so that those rulers, public officials, or political groups who commit such a crime may be punished. Besides, in the light of various resolutions of the Security Council, Hindus exodus and ethnic cleansing through terror is a crime against humanity and can lead to the trial of responsible state and not state actors under the international justice mechanism.

Ethnically discriminative Sindh Local Government Act (SPLGA)

Thirty and one days of October 2012 have shook Sindh with massive outpour and pubic disgruntlement that have led ethnic Sindhi people of the province to the streets in hundreds of thousands, caused street gun battles, murder of at least four civilians by law enforcing agencies and private armed persons and detention of 1500 protestors. At least three successful province wide shutter-down and vehicles-jam strikes were reported. The law, being ethnically discriminative, violates the indigenous majority population's right to equal participation in the governance, development and right to rule their historical motherland. It mainly is in violation of International Convention on the Elimination of All Forms of Racial Discrimination (ICERD); International Covenant on Civil and Political Rights (ICCPR) and International Convention for the Protection of All Persons from Enforced Disappearance (ICPPED).

In ICCPR, term 'racial discrimination' means any form of distinction, exclusion, restriction or preference based on race, color, descent, or national or ethnic origin which has the purpose or effect of nullifying or impairing the recognition, enjoyment or exercise, on an equal footing, of human rights and fundamental freedoms in the political, economic, social, cultural or any other field   of   public   life.

If roughly reviewed, the SPLGA is a clear violation of Article 1 (4) and Article 2(1) of ICERD, which if read in association with various concerned articles and clause of ICCPR, CECR, and ICPPED, will fall in the high degree crimes and discrimination against humanity. Article 1 (4) of ICERD reads:

> "Special measures taken for the sole purpose of securing adequate advancement of certain racial or ethnic groups or individuals requiring such protection as may be necessary in order to ensure such groups or individuals equal enjoyment or exercise of human rights and fundamental freedoms shall not be deemed racial discrimination, provided, however, that such measures do not, as a consequence, lead to the maintenance of separate rights for different racial groups and that they shall not be continued after the objectives for which they were taken have been achieved."

Whereas the various clause of Article 2 (1) reads:

> States Parties condemn racial discrimination and undertake to pursue by all appropriate means and without delay a policy of eliminating racial discrimination in all its forms and promoting understanding among all races, and, to this end: (a) Each State Party undertakes to engage in no act or practice of racial discrimination against persons, groups of persons or institutions and to ensure that all public

authorities and public institutions, national and local, shall act in conformity with this obligation; (b) Each State Party undertakes not to sponsor, defend or support racial discrimination by any persons or organizations; (c) Each State Party shall take effective measures to review governmental, national and local policies, and to amend, rescind or nullify any laws and regulations which have the effect of creating or perpetuating racial discrimination wherever it exists; (d) Each State Party shall prohibit and bring to an end, by all appropriate means, including legislation as required by circumstances, racial discrimination by any persons, group or organization; (e) Each State Party undertakes to encourage, where appropriate, integrationist multiracial organizations and movements and other means of eliminating barriers between races, and to discourage anything which tends to strengthen racial division.

Numerous clause of Sindh People's Local Government Act violate the spirit as well as various articles and clauses of ICERD. SPLGA if combined with the policies restricting Sindhi students right to study in the educational institutions as well as filters in ethnic Sindhis employment opportunities is a higher form of discrimination. Apart from administratively dividing Sindh, SPLGA ethnically discriminates through: a) resisting the process of urbanization and economic development of ethnic Sindhi population within and outside Karachi by limiting their movement and rights to the secondary and tertiary cities of the provinces; b) legalizes hegemony and monopoly of selective minority ethnic group over the majority indigenous population as well as other inhabitants of Karachi city, 3) violates ethnic Sindhi population's right to education, economic opportunities and cultural development.

Article 2 of the ICERD reads:

"States Parties shall, when the circumstances so warrant, take, in the social, economic, cultural and other fields, special and concrete measures to ensure the adequate development and protection of certain racial groups or individuals belonging to them, for the purpose of guaranteeing them the full and equal enjoyment of human rights and fundamental freedoms. These measures shall in no case entail as a consequence the maintenance of unequal or separate rights for different racial groups after the objectives for which they were taken have been achieved."

Pakistan has already signed to adhere not to practice "racial segregation and apartheid and undertake to prevent, prohibit and eradicate all practices of this nature in territories under their jurisdiction." According to Article 4 (b) and (c) of the convention, Pakistan is bound to declare those organizations illegal, and prohibit the organizations that propagate activities advocating racial discrimination, and participation in such organizations or activities as an offence punishable by law. It is also bound to disallow public authorities or public institutions to promote or incite racial discrimination.

If certain clauses of SPLGA are taken into consideration along with the ethnically selective targeted killings in the city as well other discriminative steps by Sindh Government, a high degree of civil and political violence would be evident. There are already some published election monitoring and observation documents by the Pakistani civil society that reports the violence and fabricated votes in some of the Karachi constituencies, which give edge to the an ethnic organization winning seats from the city undemocratically.

According to Article 5 (b) of ICERD:

> The right to security of person and protection by the State against violence or bodily harm, whether inflicted by government officials or by any individual group or institution; (c) Political rights, in particular the right to participate in elections-to vote and to stand for election-on the basis of universal and equal suffrage, to take part in the Government as well as in the conduct of public affairs at any level and to have equal access to public service; (d) Other civil rights, in particular..(i) The right to freedom of movement and residence within the border of the State..(e) Economic, social and cultural rights, in particular: (i) The rights to work, to free choice of employment, to just and favorable conditions of work, to protection against unemployment, to equal pay for equal work, to just and favorable remuneration;(iii) The right to housing...

Besides, according to the Article 7 of the convention Pakistan has to undertake immediate and effective measures in the fields of teaching, education, culture, and information to combat racial discrimination. It is also bound to promote understanding, tolerance, and friendship among nations and racial or ethnical groups.

The people of Sindh legitimately can approach the international legal framework in a vast arena through the various components of international legal framework, for which Article 15 (1) of the ICERD refers:

> Pending the achievement of the objectives of the Declaration on the Granting of Independence to Colonial Countries and Peoples, contained in General Assembly resolution 1514 (XV) of 14 December 1960, the provisions of this Convention shall in no way limit the right of petition granted to these peoples by other international instruments or by the United Nations and its specialized agencies.

The discrimination regarding employment in Karachi as well as education policies of academic institutions in the city can be seen in contradiction with the article 6 (2) of International Covenant on Economic, Social and Cultural Rights (ICESCR). Besides, according to Article 13 (b) and (c) secondary and higher education in all of its forms shall be made equally accessible to all.

If all these treaties are read in the context of SPLGA with the background of Declaration on the Rights of Indigenous Peoples (DRIP), this law extremely negates the internal rights regime.

According to the Article 7 (2) indigenous peoples have the collective right to live in freedom, peace, and security as distinct peoples and shall not be subjected to any act of genocide or any other act of violence. Article 8 abstains their forced assimilation or destruction of their culture and makes bound the States to prevent as well as redress their cultural values, ethnic identities, control over land as well as (geographical) territories, their forced transfer or migration from any part of their historical land and other (natural) resources (like coasts, rivers, lakes etc), as well as "any form of propaganda designed to promote or incite racial or ethnic discrimination directed against them".

Article 10 of the declaration abstains their forcibly removal from their lands or territories. According to the Article 15 (2) "States shall take effective measures, in consultation and cooperation with the indigenous peoples concerned, to combat prejudice and eliminate discrimination and to promote tolerance, understanding and good relations among indigenous peoples and all other segments of society."

According to Article 26 (1) (2) and (3) indigenous peoples have the right to own, use, develop, and control the lands, territories, and resources, which they have traditionally owned, occupied or otherwise used or acquired and States are bound to ensure this. Article 32 (1) reaffirms that indigenous peoples have the right to determine and develop priorities and strategies for the development or use of their lands or territories and other resources.

Involuntarily disappearances

The September 2012 visit of UN mission on Involuntary Disappearances of Sindh and Balochistan province to hold meetings with the political parties, civil society groups, and families of victims in which the cases and details of thousands of abducted activists were highlighted.

International Convention for the Protection of All Persons from Enforced Disappearance (ICPPED) categorically ensure binding on the signatory countries to abstain any form of enforced disappearance by the state agents or the groups in any circumstances including war, threat of war or internal political instability. The act is termed criminal and a widespread and systematic practice of disappearance is a crime against humanity and is applicable / punishable under international law according to Articles 1, 2, 4 and 5.

If only three currently highly discussed issues of Hindu exodus; ethnic discrimination and cleansing; and enforced disappearances are reviewed, one of the severe most crime against humanity in South Asia is being held with the Sindhi people. The case of Balochistan is also similar.

Conclusion
Pakistan, basically, is undergoing the state crises. It has attempted

a chemistry change in the nature of the state apparatus. State, globally, is considered a power structure of a country, which has legitimacy to use the violence through certain law enforcing agencies for maintenance of peace and civil order. The crises in Pakistan is that besides undergoing six decades of ethnic, linguistic and religious discriminations in almost all individual, social, political, economic and cultural aspects, it has shared its legitimacy to use violence with the non-state actor that carry the ethnic, racial and religious discrimination and almost virtual apartheid. This is high time when along with the legal framework, Pakistan need to undo all the gross right violations against millions of ethnic nationalities of Sindhi, Baloch and Pashtun as well as religious minorities of Pakistan. The role of Pakistani and global civil society and actor becomes crucial here.

Published on www.merinews.com on November 03, 2012

Whom Does Hindu Exodus Benefit In Pakistan?

Hindu Exodus has created a new debate around minority rights in Pakistan. Analyzing factors and repercussions as well as identifying losers-beneficiaries matrix can lead to understand the scenario ousting the indigenous community from their land.

Beginning of the Hindu exodus last week proved to be a shaker of the governance foundations in Pakistan. The government (in August 2012), on one hand, rushed to resist a possible mass exodus, and on the other, it adopted denial jargons through its Interior Ministry and Sindh Government.

Exodus of Hindus from Sindh province, Pakistan is not an abrupt reaction of some action. In fact, a gradual exodus has been in the process since 1970s after the first and historically well discussed Hindu exodus during the partition of united India.

This gradual exodus is the result of multipronged policy of Pakistani governance structure to terrorize Hindus of Sindh so that their upper cast as well as elite and middle class especially from north of Sindh may migrate to India and elsewhere. Meanwhile, the poor and Dalit Hindus who are in majority population in the Southeast could either be converted to Islam through various Islamic Missionaries and Madersahs of Wahabism as well as Devband schools of thought. Hundreds of Madersas are operating in the India-bordering districts of Umerkot, Mithi, Sanghar and Ghotki - where majority of the Pakistani Hindus dwell.

The cases of forced conversions, abductions, assassinations, and forced marriages of Hindu girls have increased over last two decades in similar pattern to the increase of Madersahs. This is a beginning of Talbanization in Sindh, which is the only secular province of Pakistan and until now has protected its Sufi - secular credentials and defended itself against religious extremism.

There are some political factors also behind this. Hindu majority of Pakistan is traditional voter of Pakistan People's Party (PPP), which is a liberal center-left populist party; therefore, the security establishment has always eyed it. Exodus of Hindus from Sindh can weaken PPP in at least ten districts of Sindh.

Besides, there are some other more important factors as well. Punjab is thickly populated province of Pakistan. It always has been shifting its populations to the rest provinces of the country and abroad. Meanwhile, emerging Punjabi and Pashtun trader and businesspersons needs new markets of investment. Khyber Pakhtunkhwa (KPK) and Balochistan are undergoing insurgency; however markets, trade and business in the majority districts of Sindh is led by Hindu mercantile, entrepreneur and investor. The exodus will serve the population and business interests of Punjab and KPK. It will also lead to the first success of Taliban in Sindh. More horrific is the fact that it will convert Sindhi indigenous population of the province into the permanent minority in their historical land.

Sindhi feudal class no doubt is monstrous but has never been fanatic. Its majority is still secular; however, those who are weaker in power in their constituencies, have aligned with the Mullahs. The emerging Sindhi middle class as well as traditional feudal in association with civil society, media and political parties including Sindhi nationalists have rejuvenated the Hindu rights and protection movement in Sindh after the hype of Hindu Exodus because they are secular and more then that it is in their political and ethnic interests.

Exodus is none's interest -- neither India, nor Pakistan and Sindh. The only missing link is the realization of necessary change on the part of establishment. What is to be done then? The only way is the ruling elites and establishment of Pakistan need to review the country's policies, legal framework, and so-called ideological notion towards Hindus and other minorities. If they kept on avoiding this noble task, time and nature will avoid them for sure.

Published on www.merinews.com on August 20, 2012

Vernacular Media under Siege in Pakistan

Pakistan is a virtual hell for the free, neutral, bold and intellectually sound media-associated persons and journalists, especially the associates of vernacular Sindhi and Baloch media. Dozens of media-associated persons and opinion makers are victimized or killed by the military, Inter-Service-Intelligence (ISI) and Military Intelligence (MI) as well as their supported urban or religious terrorists. Given the exclusive *Punjabization* of almost every civil and military institution of Pakistan, there has been no single quotable case of the murder and/or brutalization of a Punjabi journalist from 1947 to 2013. Saleem Shahzad and Najam Sethi were exceptions because Shahzad touched the forbidden tree - the evidence of the nexus between Islamist terrorists and the garrison city Rawalpindi, and Najam Sethi held secular views and opposed the Punjabi military establishment of Pakistan. (However, today, he is also closely linked with the military establishment unlike his wonderful past).

It is condemnable that Raza Rumi and Hamid Mir (although both Punjabi journalists well known for their deep roots in the military establishment) were attacked before and after the visit of Committee for the Protection of Journalists (CPJ) in Pakistan. CPJ was worried about victimization and murders of journalists in Pakistan since Baloch and Sindhi and to certain extent Pashtun journalists from Sindh and Balochistan have been victims.

It is an irony that Pakistan's so-called Urdu and English national media has been reluctant to publish or telecast the news about the abduction and murder of Sindhi and Baloch journalists and human rights activists. The criminal silence adopted by the All Pakistan Newspapers Society (APNS), Pakistan Federal Union of Journalist

(PFUJ) and South Asia Free Media Association (SAFMA) Pakistan Chapter over the victimization of Sindhi and Baloch journalists has been disastrous. Unfortunately, at the behest of Punjabi power, ethnicity has trumped the sanctity of humanity in Pakistan to the point that murder and persecution of Sindhi and Baloch journalists and human rights defenders gets hardly any space in the leading English and Urdu media of Pakistan.

Media freedom then and now

In Pakistan, the media has a limited freedom within the parameters narrowly described by the powerful military establishment of the country concerning professional activities including reporting, publishing, analyzing, writing and opinionating.

If seen from the evolutionary perspective of media freedom, Pakistani media has undergone four phases of transformation. During the country's first three decades (1947 – 1979), Pakistani media enjoyed a greater degree of freedom across the country at the national level, but was less free at the rural level. The crucial period for freedom of press was that of the military rule of General Ziaulhaq (1980 – 1988), when media faced severe curbs to appropriately reporting and opinionating about the democratic movement whose centre-stage was Sindh. Media got breathing space only once again during a decade of elected civil governance (1988 – 1998). A relatively higher degree of freedom at every level under civilian governments was enjoyed. The worst media curbs ever imposed were during the rule of General Pervaiz Musharaf (1999 – 2008). He induced deceptive policies. His policies for virtually controlling media were under cover of freedom of media. The General used media camouflage; however, he imposed curbs and censures on the freedom of Sindhi and Balochi media. The virtual censure he imposed is still in the place.

Militarization of media

The media, especially Sindhi and Baloch media, face major challenges in their professional endeavors from various corners, including state institutions as well as state- supported non-state actors.

The military establishment led by Pakistan's Army - particularly that part engaged in military and/or clandestine operations in

Sindh and Baluchistan through its intelligence wings like ISI and MI with the technical help of Inter Service Public Relation (ISPR)- is led by a Major General level senior military official assisted by a fleet of Captain-Major-Colonel journalists, reporters, editors and directors of media houses. Their task has been to determine the level of coverage for particular events, news, or political parties; controlling Op-Ed pages; introducing pitches against civil governments and controlling media coverage of secessionist movements in Sindh and Balochistan.

Freedom in chains

The Pakistani military has had a separate and highly specialized cell for Balochi, Sindhi and Pashtun media since 2000, when the military started inviting journalists from across the Pakistan to establish military-media courting relations to woo dominant civil thought. The unwritten dirty media policy imposed on Sindhi media had verbal instructions like (i) use the word "law enforcement agency" instead of "Pakistan Army" if the military attacks citizens in Sindh and Balochistan or the citizens from these province protest against the army's atrocities; (ii) use word "elder province" instead of "Punjab" if there is a protest or statement against Punjab; and (iii) use word "Aajpo" (salvation) instead of "Azad" (freedom) when news of secessionist activity is published. These procedures were advised (i.e. instructed) in meetings with editors by the "Date Offices" as ISI and MI call their Public Relations offices established in every Sub-district (Tehsil), District and Division headquarter.

Forced Salafization

In a bid to Salafize the masses, especially the secular and liberal Sindhi and Baloch, the pseudo-secular and unenlightened as well as non-moderation policy of General Musharaf asked the vernacular media (which attracts the largest audiences) not to publish words like "Khuda" and "Maseet," which are local names in Sindhi, Balochi, Siraki and Punjabi for "God" and "Mosque." Instead, they were instructed to publish words "Allah" and "Masjid" - the Arabic version. This was in bid to Salafize Sindhi, Baloch and Siraki societies.

Security-mafia control

After the Great Flood of the Indus in 2010, the media was pressured not to quote the actual number of victims as well as the velocity of the disaster. This was a taboo for the area of security installations as well as for Sindh and Balochistan.

On the other hand, in cities, the militant wings of the political - particularly ethnic - parties as in Karachi often harass journalists if their work challenges the interests of these powerful groups / individuals. These groups had the military establishment's support. The murder of journalist Wali Khan Babar and the attack on the office of AAJ TV in Karachi by a party allied to General Pervaiz Musharaf are the much-quoted examples of this.

Journalism in danger

Journalists in Pakistan face various kinds of dangers. Abduction as well as killing of journalists and analysts by the military and other armed forces like the Pakistan Rangers (in Sindh), Front Constabulary (Balochistan), Frontiers Force (Khyber Pakhtunkhuwa) as well as local police has been reported since the 1980s and especially after 2000. On the other hand, the enforced disappearance and torture of reporters and analysts by the intelligence agencies especially ISI and MI has been a major problem of the last decade and is ongoing. The worst condition is the targeted killing and in some cases poisoning of journalists. Targeted killing of journalists by the militant wings of an ethnic political party in Karachi and some exceptional cases in the countryside by the powerful landholders has been reported at various times.

On the other hand, pressure looms large on the media houses to sack reporters and Op-editors / columnists / contributors if they go beyond the limits devised by the security establishment. Poisoning of journalists, writers and columnists, in cases where their abduction or murder would become a matter of public outcry has also been attempted in some cases over the last decade.

Economic punishments

Government advertisements are stopped and private entrepreneurs pressured to discourage advertising in targeted media houses, if they do not comply with the orders of the Pakistan Army and its associated security agencies.

Pakistan imports paper for printing and has a subsidized quota for each print media house. When a media house does not comply with the instructions of the civil government or the military establishment, its quota is challenged.

What is to be done?

Legislation clearly devising a framework of freedom for working journalists, including staffers, reporters, correspondents, analysts, anchorpersons, Op-ed teams and columnists as well as freelancers must be enacted. Moreover, provincial / federal level tribunals should be established in case the freedom of professional activity for print, electronic and social media is circumscribed. In case of harassment, particularly murder or attempted murder, an inquiry commission should be formed that must contain persons not only from Pakistan, but also observers from the international network. Moreover, relevant amendments should be made in the Criminal Procedure Code and other legal frameworks for mentioning the procedure and punishment term if a journalist, opinion maker, columnist, analyst, anchorperson or social media activist is harassed, tortured, or killed. Furthermore, a permanent international commission should be created to carry out inquiries as well as generate political pressure if media associates are targeted in civil-war laden countries like Pakistan, Afghanistan, and Syria etc.

On the other hand, social media have mostly been trying to focus on what the so-called national media, as well as corporate media have been unable to do due to their own policies and/or pressure from the authorities. The role of social media has been positive in Pakistan, as proven during the 2013 elections when social media activists / citizen-journalists uncovered election irregularities, due to which the Election Commission of Pakistan (ECP) announced re-elections in some of electoral constituencies.

Making political parties accountable has been a great failure of Pakistani media - particularly the electronic media - as most of the time some select individuals or specific political parties are made the sole focus of accountability – generally as a result of big media houses' bias or the pressure from their friendly association with the military establishment. In fact, holding Pakistani politicians accountable is not a problematic affair per se for the Pakistani media; however, media mostly avoid holding accountable those politicians and religious party leaders who have the power to make violence, have military backing, or are part of the military itself.

The primary issue in Pakistan is holding the military establishment of the country accountable for its unnecessary interference in civilian domains, especially the vernacular media of Sindh and Balochistan.

Published on Truthout, USA on July 26, 2014

Does a 2011 Terrorist Episode Foreshadow the Talibanization of Sindh?

On November 07, 2011, in Chak town of district Shikarpur in Sindh, Pakistan, four armed men said to be religious extremists entered the Otaq (a traditional community gathering place in rural Sindh) of Dr. Satya Pal and opened fire on several Hindus, Dr. Ajeet Kumar; Ashoke Kumar (an Income Tax Officer); Naresh Kumar; and Dr. Satya Pal. Naresh Kumar and Ashok Kumar died on the spot, while Dr. Ajeet breathed his last in the Civil Hospital of Sukkur city; while Dr. Satya Paul survived, albeit with severe injuries. He was hospitalized in Agha Khan University Hospital in Karachi. According to the single witness, the attackers fled to the nearby Indus river forests. The issue created fury among residents of the area as well as across Sindh and caused public unrest. This is the first reported attack against a religious minority in Sindh since the partition of India in 1947.

Civil society activists of Hyderabad formed a fact-finding team on the direction of Mr. Amarnath Motumal, vice chairperson, Human Rights Commission of Pakistan (HRCP) Sindh Chapter, which included this writer; however HRCP did not accept the report, and it was therefore not made public.

Socio-cultural Outlook of the Crime Scene

At least one century old, the Sindh town of Chak is situated on the western bank of the Indus River in the Shikarpur district of Sindh, Pakistan, one of the districts nearest to Pakistan's largest military installation in Pano Aqil town. It is an economic, educational, social, and transport hub for the adjoining towns and villages of the district and home to a population of more than 40,000, out of which 6,000 are Hindu, with the remainder Sunni and Shia

Muslim. The Mehar and Bhaya communities of the indigenous Sindhis inhabit the town in majority.

Agriculture, retail shops, jobs in government and private organizations are the sources of livelihood for residents. The town is the nearest market for Indus forest inhabitants. Eight major primary, secondary and higher secondary boys and girls schools and three major libraries are the source of youth literacy and socio-political consciousness. A popular secular Sindhi Literary magazine, "Sindhu," once published from here a couple of decades ago. Until the recent past, there were no traces of religious hatred or extremism. Hazrat Humbah is the shrine of the leading Sufi saint in the area. Hindus and Muslims pay homage to this Muslim Sufi saint together.

Exceptional as well as unexpected to the common Sindhi consciousness and mindset, there are at least seven Madrasas in the town, five of which belong to Jamiat-e-Ulmai-e-Islam (JUI) (three for men and two for women), one each associated with Jamiat-e-Ulmai-e-Pakistan (JUP) and Fiqa-e-Jafferia (FeJ). A couple of other unregistered Madrasas are also in operation here. Hizbul Ibrar is a 40-year-old madrasahs. Locals say that a considerable number of people in the area are also associated with Sipah-e-Sahaba Pakistan (SSP) and Lashkar-e-Jhangvi (LeJ), banned religious militant outfits supported by the security establishment of Pakistan and widely believed by Pakistanis to have links with Taliban, al-Qaeda and Lashkar-e-Tayyaba (LeT).

A majority of the Mehar Muslim and Hindu communities are traditional voters for Sardar Ghous Bux Mahar, while the second majority vote goes to the Bhaya clan's chief, Sardar Wahid Bux Bhayo and his nephew Babul Khan Bhayo. Polling results in the last three decades show that Sardar Ghous Bux Mahar has always won the polling station here. Many political parties, including the Pakistan People's Party (PPP), Jeay Sindh Qomi Mahaz (JSQM), Sindh Taraqi Passand Party (STP), Pakistan Muslim League - Q (PML - Q), and some other liberal and secular parties as well have local branches. According to local journalists, two minor incidents of Hindu victimization occurred from 1980 to 2000.

Commoners' opinions

According to commoners associated with the Bhaya, Mehar, Channa and other clans, Hindu and Muslims have been living in peaceful coexistence here for decades. The opening of the Madrasas in the town has torn the fabric of harmony, peace and tranquility. According to them, Qazi Ghulam Mohammad Bhayo (a Sipah-e-Sahaba associate), Molvi Ahsan Bhayo (JUI - F) and Abdul Ghani Bhayo have been the actors inciting religious hatred in the area. They also told our commission that one Seema Bhayo, who was having a love affair with the one of the murdered Hindus, was missing after the Diwali (Festival of Lights) day incident. They speculated that she most probably was illegally confined in the custody of the Mehar clan's chieftain.

Some of the people said that two days after the murders, on the morning of November 9, 2011, Ghous Bux Mahar visited the town and inquired publicly, over the Holy Book of Quran (a normal traditional ritual), about the identity of the murderers. A person stood up and identified culprits Iqbal Bhayo and Islam Bhayo. The former was a retired Pakistan Army soldier.

Journalists speak

The journalists of the Chak and Press Club Sukkur were of the opinion that the incident resulted from the nexus of the mullahs and the military, with support from the local feudal chief. They were of the opinion that the event was not an honor killing, but a well-planned act of terrorism serving the interests of the mullah, military and feudal nexus in northern Sindh. They were of the opinion that the weaker political players had facilitated the incident to claim their hold on votes by instigating religious conflict.

What did the victims' families say?

The family members of the victims refused to discuss the details of the event, however, they said that Mukhi of their Panchayat would talk on their behalf. Mukhi Premchand of Chak Panchyat said that on behalf of Hindu Panchayat, he went to the elders of the various communities regarding the Diwali day issue. He said that the triple murder was an act of terrorism.

What actually happened?

According local journalists, after the Diwali incident, Qazi Ghulam Mohammad Bhayo, a local leader of Sipah-e-Sahaba (SSP) contacted Babal Khan Bhayo to take the girl Seema away from the town. Local sources from the Bhayo community claim the guards of Babal Khan Bhayo came to Nazeer Mahar's house to pick the girl up. Seema's father refused them and told them that the issue had been misreported to the community chieftain. He told them that the girl was not inside the house, but was attending class at school. They dismissed the poor Nazir Mahar's plea and kidnapped Seema and handed her over to the Babul Khan Bhayo. Since then, the girl has been missing, and her father Nazeer Mahar is not willing to speak with journalists and human rights activists.

According to the villagers, a few days before the incident, activists of the JUI and SSP also made public funds collection drive in the area for Jihad in the district. After the incidents, local police raided the houses of various suspects, but a group of religious zealots mobbed the local police station and chanted slogans against the police and in favor of Jihad. The villagers also said that the families of the victims have been threatened not to pursue the case.

Police version

Local police claimed that Inspectors Ghulam Nabi and Ghulam Ali received injuries from crossfire during the raid on the suspects' homes. When asked why the Police Picket (the police post installed in the village for the security of residents) was not staffed on the day of the terrorist event - which otherwise, according to residents, used to be posted in the town - he said due to *Eid-ul-Zuha* holidays, the personnel were home. We asked a police official which religious organizations are active in the town. JUI and SSP, he replied. We told him that SSP is a banned outfit. He kept silent.

According to the police, they charged Ehsan Bhayo, Abdul Ghani, Abdul Lateef, Abdul Rauf and others under sections 353, 302, and 324 of the Criminal Procedure Code of Pakistan.

The deputy inspector general of Sindh Police Larkana zone, Sain Rakhyo Mirani, said in an interview by a Sindhi daily Sham (newspaper) that the incident was part of a series of harassment activities against Hindus in Sindh.

Attempting Talibanization

The incident of Chak was probably the first of its kind in Sindh after the creation of Pakistan, which is indicative of inroads by the Taliban in the province. The incident suggests that the security establishment of Pakistan wants to Talibanize Sindh. It is appropriately feared by the people that Talbanization of Sindh would further destabilize South Asia. We called for a protest against the incident that was well received and thousands took to the street in Sindh. The time has come that the international community and the world citizenry need to think about Sindh!

Published in Truthout, USA November 22, 2013

Suspicious Details Emerge after Three Men Burned Alive in Pakistan

Numbers can be affecting. It is shocking indeed to learn through the reports of Amnesty International and Human Rights Watch that at least 861 persons were disappeared by security agencies in Pakistan during 2012; around 325 Shia minority persons were killed on sectarian grounds; and around 100 were extra-judicially killed by the military officials. These numbers do not include the thousands who lost their lives in Balochistan and Sindh in military actions during the past decade.

What pierces through the deepest core of a human heart about the rights violations are the stories, which unfold, as numbers cannot, the real level and nature of brutalities. A single instance is enough to portray the truth about the so-called internal national security and sovereignty notions of a federation like Pakistan, where the terms "security" and "sovereignty" apply to geography only - not to the people.

On the sunny Thursday of April 21, 2011, Pakistani electronic media carried breaking news of the burning alive of three Sindhi nationalist leaders - Qurban Khuhawar, Ruplo Cholyani and Nadir Bugti - in Sindh's Shanghar district by unknown assailants. The victims were associated with Jeay Sindh Mutahida Mahaz (JSMM) - a political organization advocating Sindh independence recently banned by Pakistan authorities. All of the victims, the report said, were sitting in the car, which was torched on a country road.

After a few days, we formed a fact-finding mission of rights activists, journalists, and academicians to inquire into the incident on the behalf of the Human Rights Commission of Pakistan. It was a drive of 117 kilometers of curvy road from Hyderabad, the second-largest city of Sindh, amid the mixed texture of green pastures and sand dunes on the roadsides. The place where the incident occurred was 7.5 kilometers from Sanghar town on the Sanghar-Khipro road and was between Bakhoro Bridge and Mithrau Canal Bridge - historical sites where, during early 1940s, a Sindhi Hur guerrilla army was stationed fighting British troops for the freedom of Sindh. A small bazaar runs between both bridges with a couple of dozen shops and tea vendors. The distance between the bridges is 1 kilometer.

We started mingling with the people regarding the incident. Eyewitnesses told us that the incident took place by 1:30 PM. According to them, a couple of hours before arrival of the ambushed, extraordinary movement by a black car and a military green jeep were observed.

Both vehicles, the onlookers said, were positioned near Mithrau Bridge earlier and started blocking and diverting the vehicular traffic. Furthermore, people were asked to stay in the bazaar until told otherwise. As soon as the victims' car (ARW 028), hailing from Sanghar, crossed the Bakhoro Bridge, a white car was already chasing them. It blinked the front lights near Bakhoro Bridge and turned away. Swiftly thereafter, a red double cabin Jeep already positioned at the bridge moved toward the victims' car. A car from the Bakhoro Bridge side also reached there. According to the peasants in the nearby fields, both vehicles opened fire from automatic guns on the victims' car from two directions.

The victims' car lost the track and fell in the ditch near cultivated fields. According to the peasants working in nearby fields, the assailants, in military camouflage as well as in plainclothes, disembarked from the vehicles and opened fire over the car again. They also threw small plastic bags on the car. Witnesses said the car caught fire from various directions immediately after the bags were thrown.

Fifteen men remained at the site for around ten minutes after torching the car, said Juman Leghari - a peasant from nearby village Maulvi Kher Mohammad Ahmedani. Six or seven were in commando camouflage, and the others were in plainclothes, he added. Once the assailants left, bystanders rushed to the car.

Shortly thereafter, a black car reached the scene from the direction of Sanghar; people in the car fired shots into the air, and the car drove away. Police reached the scene afterward. Bystanders wanted to fight the fire, but the police did not allow them to. In the meantime, a person cried from the torched car that he was alive and begged for his rescue, Muharram said with tears in eyes. "As we rushed to him, police officials stopped us by shouting that the ambushed persons were terrorists." At this point, the victim later identified as Noorullah Tunio said they were Sindhi nationalists and that the Punjabi (Pakistani) Army had attacked them. Thereafter, the people pushed the police officials back and rescued him. According to the person who rescued him, Tunio crawled out of the car, put mud on the burnt lower part of body and chanted slogans for the freedom of Sindh. The villagers escorted Tunio on a motorcycle rickshaw to the hospital in Sanghar.

We met constable Bachal Dars and others at the police post. They told us that no one was at the police post at the time of incident because they had been sent by higher-ups to a nearby school where examinations were being held. According to them, as soon as they learned about the incident, they informed the station house police officer; however, he instructed them to stay in the school.

The shopkeepers of the bazaar said no arms were found in the vehicle. They said it was an assault, not an encounter, because only the armed forces opened fire.

The people told us that they contacted the Edhi Foundation for an ambulance, but it reached the scene after 90 minutes. The Edhi Foundation representative in Sanghar, Ashraf Hussain, showed us the record carrying invoice number 837737, which said an ambulance (PA 3355) was sent to the location at 3 PM. Area residents also kept calling the police helpline, but police who reached the scene tried to stop the people from rescuing the only survivor.

On the way back to Sanghar, we examined the torched car in the local police station and found at least 24 bullet holes in it; however, the vehicle's compressed natural gas-petroleum cylinder and petrol tank were intact. The police registered case FIR 96/2011 of April 25 after five days of incidents. The deputy superintendent of police, Sanghar Ghulam Shabir, said the victims were against Pakistan and therefore very bad persons. While asked about the police action for identification and detention of the culprits, he said that they had managed to flee.

Dr. Abdul Razzaq Leghari of the Sanghar civil hospital said 60 percent of Tunio's body was burned. He also said the arms and leg bones of the persons sitting in the front seats could not be found from their ashes. This created doubts regarding the use of chemicals in the bags thrown upon the victims' car. Medico Legal Officer Dr. Shabir Cheema said the way security agencies were pressuring him was indicative of their involvement in the assault.

Local journalists told us that the news they released was not carried by the country's mainstream English print and electronic media; however, a distorted news story released from the city of Mirpurkhas, some 40 kilometers away, was carried by those outlets.

Pakistan's Prime Minister took the notice of the carnage and asked Chief Minister Sindh to order an inquiry. All other political parties demanded a judicial inquiry. No official inquiry has taken place since 2011.

Finally, Tunio was shifted to Civil Hospital Karachi on the same day and later on to the Patel Hospital, where he died May 1, 2011. Before his death, he said the ISI and Pakistan Army's commandos ambushed him and his comrades.

The details of the incident portray Pakistan's government's approach toward political dissent. It also is indicative of unnecessary and unlawful use of militarization in Sindh and Balochistan. Worst of all was the silence of Pakistan's human rights ministry.

This was not an isolated incident. Hundreds of such incidents have taken place mostly in Sindh and Balochistan in the past three decades. While discussing Pakistan, it is important to note that human rights violations there have an exclusive peculiarity: state organs and their proxy non-state elements jointly plan and effect heinous crimes against humanity. It is not the legal framework alone that must be changed; it is the nature of statehood and its ethnic chemistry that needs to be altered.

No other state like Pakistan has shared its statehood characteristics of legitimacy over the use of violence with non-state actors. Such non-state actors have been known to kidnap and forcibly convert Hindu and Christian minority girls as well as to harass these communities through Pakistan's notorious blasphemy law. The trigger-happy state security outfits disappear and extra-judicially kill activist citizens and use the virtual means of ethnic cleansing that have been adopted in Sindh and Balochistan. This is the time when humanity on globe should think seriously about the 70 million Sindhi and Balochistani of Pakistan.

Published in Truthout, USA on July 20, 2013

Roots of Sindhi-Hindu Exodus from Pakistan

The morning of August 10, 2012 carried news of exodus of Hindus from Pakistan. Immigration authorities detained 250 families having valid documents and visas at Wagha-Atari border of India and Pakistan near Lahore. Later on, they were allowed to travel to India after signing commitment bonds for returning. More families thereafter have also left Pakistan for India.

The news went viral. Media on either side of the border ran heated debates on the issue which occupied the front pages of many dailies for the next three days. Pakistan's Interior Minister, Rehman Malik tuned the same old mantra of 'Indian conspiracy against Pakistan'. President Asif Zardari immediately formed a three-member committee of parliamentarians to resist possibilities of an exodus. They held meetings with the Hindu community leaders and civil society representatives in Sukkur, Hyderabad and Karachi, but the latter declared that meetings were not enough, some concrete steps regarding the protection of Hindus and all necessary legislations should be made. Sindhi nationalists also launched a movement against forced exodus of Hindus.

Hindu Exodus is historically referred to as the mass migration of Hindus from newly formed Pakistan after partition of the Indian subcontinent on August 14, 1947. Partition is now a sixty-five years old story but it is still going on like a big-bang process. In fact, the formation of two sovereign countries out of united India under British rule on the basis of religion has vitiated the situation in Pakistan. The country has leaped one eighty degrees into religious extremism against the liberal and secular ethos of various communities mostly due to the ongoing insurgency in Afghanistan. This has made Hindus, Christian and other minorities vulnerable through the establishment supported activities of forced conversions, abductions, and plunder and life threats.

Hindus are 5.5 percent in Pakistan and most are from the indigenous population of Sindh, where they count 7 million. Several factors exist to cause a possible massive forced exodus of Sindhi Hindus. In the recent exodus attempt, authorities as well as the community numerously mentioned 'security' as a reason of exodus which if seen carefully embodies the various connotations of ideology, economy, power politics, fanaticism, feudalism and demography.

Sindh is a demographically vulnerable province of Pakistan where the indigenous Sindhi, nearly 17 percent of whom is Hindu, are facing threat of being converted into a permanent minority on their historical homeland. In August 1947, they were 98 percent of the province out of which 35 percent were Hindus. They are now reduced to 65 percent only. In fact, Sindh has become a large refugee receptor from Afghanistan, Bangladesh, Myanmar and Tribal Areas along with other three provinces of Pakistan.

The history of political and social conflicts in Pakistan is a history of the demographic conflicts based on invasions and struggles for securities among the federating states and particularly between Punjab province and the rest. It is an emerging public concern in Sindh that north of the province is being converted into the second Taliban hub of Pakistan through extraordinary support to religious extremists, frequent settlement of ethnic Pashtuns and Punjabis and increase in the anti-Hindu activities. This demographic threat has also been a major factor in harboring the recent secessionist wave among ethnic Sindhis, who, according to Pakistani English and Sindhi dailies of March 24, 2012, took to the streets of Karachi in hundreds of thousands on March 23 and demanded separation of Sindh from Pakistan. A couple of dozens of militancy incidents have been reported in the province thereafter.

The law and order situation is worst in northern Sindh since the uprising against military rule during 1980s. Sindh was non-tribal before 1990; however, its northern districts are now tribal fiefdoms. The widely considered milestone among Sindhi people for this retrogression is the establishment of Pakistan's largest cantonment in Pano Aqil, Sukkur of the northern Sindh during late 1980s. Strangely, most of the military installations in Sindh are near Hindu settlements; therefore, one assumes that a demographic strategic-security notion of the establishment might have been one factor behind displacing Hindus from there. Ironically, Hindus are being considered a demographical threat by the security establishment, majority of which considers Hindus and Indians interchangeable. Evacuee property law of the country validates this argument when it categorizes the property of Hindus who left Sindh after 1971 as an 'enemy property'.

Sindhi Hindus are a trade and business backbone of the province. Their exodus will hence create a new business space for ethnic Punjabis, Pashtuns and Urdu-speaking people. On the other hand, Sindhi feudal lords are gradually losing their economic, social and political power base; therefore, weaker among them are allying with Mullahs for their sustenance. Majority of feudal lords is traditionally secular, which was historically witnessed during the partition of India; when communal violence gripped the subcontinent, Sindh was peaceful and harmonious. However, feudal lords today are tilting towards religious extremism in northern Sindh.

After recent wave of Sindhi nationalism and freedom movement, a Hindu exodus is the most suitable for the establishment to convert ethnic Sindhis into permanent minority on their historical land, who may easily be outnumbered in any post exodus scenario by the immigrant and settler Punjabis and Pashtuns and the Urdu speaking Muhajir.

Northern Sindh, once eastern business hub of Subcontinent and housing a large number of Hindus has now become hub of Madrasahs of politically motivated and radicalbrands of fundamentalists. Being just a ten hour road journey from both Kandahar and Delhi, (if border-entry diversions are not considered),it was a trade hub with Eurasia, Central Asia and Afghanistan during early 1990s. Hindus in Sindh and particularly in its northern parts are often kidnapped, plundered, murdered and are forcedly converted to Islam by these Mullahs or their associate criminals.

At times, one finds ideological conflict as the cause of violence against the Hindus, while at others it becomes a pretext. Pakistan's civil and military bureaucracy is largely ethnic Punjabi, followed by the Pashtuns and Urdu-speaking community. Majority of the Punjabi and Urdu-speaking bureaucrats are the first or second generation of the refugees who migrated during the partition of India. Therefore, anti-Hindu mindset based on hatred caused by the violence of partition is still hounding Pakistan.

Pakistan, no doubt, desperately needs to carry on anti-Taliban campaigns at the Afghan borders; however it primarily needs to liberalize state ideology and mindset of bureaucracy; de-Talibanize Pakistani society; control radical Madrasahs, secularize academic curriculum and ensure security and equal rights to Hindus, Christians and other minority groups. It also requires urgent federal reforms, assuring demographic and ethnic sovereignty to the federating provinces. Separation of religion from the state is a prerequisite for it. Otherwise, the legacy of partition will space out too many sub-partitions in Pakistan.

Published on the website of Centre for Land Warfare Studies (CLAWS) on August 25, 2012

Personal Reflection: Politics of Development and Civil Society of Pakistan

Politics of development and particularly international development is highly complex structure of studies; however when it is attempted to understand in a very naïve way, it becomes easiest for the common understanding.

Being associated with the human rights, journalism and development sector during my career time in Pakistan, I have a few simple readings, observations, feelings and understandings of practical political aspects of development and rights based activism and their funder nexus. I am sharing these briefly and in simple manner avoiding the larger academic discussion and discourse around the development politics in Pakistan.

In Pakistan, the leadership of development and rights based initiatives is primarily dominated by ethnic Punjabis, together with their ethnic Urdu speaking as well as to some extent their sycophants from Hazara division in Khyber Pakhtunkhuwa. The visible participation of Sindhi and Baloch civil society leadership at the Central level is as unimaginable as their visibility in Pakistan's military and civil bureaucracy and the security fraternity.

Pakistan has been reluctant to include Sindhi and Baloch into cricket and other sports team, therefore, the popular and sarcastic name of 'Pakistan Eleven' team by people of Sindh and Balochistan is 'Punjab Eleven' although the team accommodates a few Urdu speaking and Pashtuns players as well. No Sindhi and Baloch cricketer has been taken in the team in last three decades.

It is worth mentioning that a high quality cricket team of Sindh was there before partition of India, which played many matches with internationals teams, the popular of which was the match between the teams of Australia and Sindh held on November 22, 1935 that was won by Sindh team comprising Hindu and Muslim Sindhis. The match held in Karachi attracted at least five thousand viewers at that time.

The civil society initiatives, human rights activism, and development politics in Pakistan have similar trends of ethnic composition of almost every state and non-state institution. Punjabis and their Urdu speaking junior partners, and a smaller quantity of the Pashtun and Hindko speaking people dominate Pakistani establishment. Similar trend is found in almost every sphere of life in Pakistan particularly of civil society, funding mainstream and flow as well as civil society leadership.

Politics behind networking

The art of networking is the modus operandi through which the powerful Punjabis, Urdu speaking and Hindko community capture the leadership of the civil society of Sindh, Siraiki South Punjab, Pakhtunkhuwa and Balochistan.

It is a strange coincidence that a large number of retired military commissioned officers have registered and are running their own NGOs, despite the fact that the top leadership of civil society in Pakistan, which mostly is Punjabi and Urdu speaking.

Most of the Pakistan level civil society leadership is Punjabi and had closely or remotely family relations with the serving or retired senior military officials who usually hold rank from Brigadiers to Lt-Generals.

Punjabis, Urdu speaking and Hindko lead the major networks of civil society organizations / Non Government Organizations (NGOs). Some Lahore, Karachi, and Quetta based organization run by Punjabis and to some extent by Urdu speaking have only one role -- they primarily establish their networks of community based organizations of Sindhis, Balochis and Sirakis; manage to elect themselves as their leader; and start owning their initiatives and market them to the donors.

Besides receiving funding, they start their networking with the world outside Pakistan, so that the image, feel, perception and the reality of Pakistan's internal society they want to show to the others may not contradict the overall foreign policy of Pakistan. Besides, by doing this, they undertake a triple advantage of acquiring central leadership role of being civil society, become the people's diplomats outside Pakistan and receiving larger international funding.

The outcome of this is propelling the softer cloud around the overall Pakistani establishment's opinion in the South Asian, continental and global civil society orbit, rights bodies and intelligentsia so that Pakistan's official opinion on internal and external affairs could be defended in a milder way. Thus, the international criticism on Pakistan is attempted to be tackled and toned down in the softer manner.

A virtual monopoly

Roughly speaking, five major civil society organizations of Pakistan are controlling, dominating, and holding the black and white of the civil society. These civil society organizations and their leadership is the heads, members and leaders of almost all civil society networks.

This include the thematic networking on the urban labor, land rights, human rights, political rights, democracy, governance, minority rights, peace and human security, India-Pakistan peace initiatives, youth networks, South Asian unity, Global South initiatives, Pakistani, South Asian, and world leftist activism, World Social Forum, flood relief, disaster management, community mobilization, election monitoring, honor killings, bonded labor rights and a vast number of other affairs.

These five plus a couple more civil society outfits represent Pakistan around the world. Their business is that the international funding, province wise donors funding flow and civil society leaderships' foreign interaction should maximally be Punjab based and Punjabi-Urdu oriented.

Donors' interests and their development politics

International interests associated with the foreign policy of the developed countries are the reason behind their funding to the developing countries. The simple, common, and naïve form of their interest is that donning country's contribution should be acknowledged in the fund-receiving countries by government, society and the civil buffer that is usually called civil society. At the end of project, program or plan, they usually demand visibility from the receiving organization so that community and / or the targeted civil society layer may keep a positive corner for the funding country. They also developed a country strategy / policy in consultation with the experts and civil society organizations so that they may strategies their funding priorities. Moreover, during the funding cycle, they collect the reports and results as well as overall outcomes of the particular funding flow.

This typical development and rights intervention planning and reporting mechanism do not only serve the monitoring and transparency requirement of a donor / project implementation process, it also give a broader feel and feedback to the funding country to assess Pakistan society, be informed on the social dynamics as well as issues. This is the point where Pakistani establishment wants the infiltration into Pakistani civil society in a manner to guide, control, and manipulates the outgoing feedback, perception, and feel.

A strange example for that is the Punjabi-Urdu-Hindko led Pakistani civil society has been transferring the messages to the most of the developed countries through development politics messaging that honor killing as well crime is the bigger problem in Sindh; honor killing, burying alive, feudalism is the major problem of Balochistan; and Talbanization is a gross level issue of Pakhtunkhuwa.

Honor killing and bonded labor is the issue of Siraiki speaking South Punjab; however police atrocities as well as right to development like health, education and poverty are the major issues in the central Punjab. Through thus, they successfully damage the image of Sindh and Balochistan where freedom movements are strong, limiting the Talibanization to Pakhtunkhuwa so that the existence of Talibanization factories in central and northern Punjab may camouflaged.

Most of the Urdu speaking civil society mention that feudalism is the biggest problem in Sindh; by saying this, they mean that Sindhis are backward, rural, and illiterate.

At South Asia level interaction, most of the civil society leadership has been creating an environment conducive to the interests of Pakistani establishment and their partner like Mutahida Qaumi Movement (MQM) and Taliban. The examples of such fallacies or propaganda can be heard easily in India, Nepal, Bangladesh, and Sri Lanka.

Here are some examples of the negative propaganda against Sindhi, Baloch and Pashtuns in South Asia spread by the civil society leadership which is known back in Pakistan as 'always-in aeroplanes':

Fallacy I: Sindhis are minority in Sindh where illiterate Sindhi feudal lords, Punjabis and military does not want Urdu speaking refugees of Indian partition to live a middle class Urban life.

Reality: Sindhis are at least 68 percent in Sindh. Urdu speaking are an ethnic minority in Karachi; however they have been taking 70 percent of economic and opportunity share of Sindh since last sixty seven years.

Fallacy II: Sindhi feudal lords harass Sindhi Hindus, they disallow them to burn their kins' dead bodies and kidnap their girls.

Reality: Sindhis and Baloch are the only ethnicities of Pakistan that support and defend as much as they can their Hindu brothers. Establishment supported Mullahs that are imported to the Saudi Arabia funded Madersas harass Sindhi Hindus. The builder mafia associated with MQM demolishes the historical villages of Hindu community in Pakistan.

Fallacy III: It was Zulfiqar Ali Bhutto, a Sindhi, who wanted military operation against Bangladesh. Punjabi and Urdu speaking have a lesser role in that.

Reality: Eighty percent of Pakistan Army is of ethnic Punjabi origin. At the time of 1971 war, they were more than ninety percent of the army. It was institutional decision of Pakistan Army to undertake   military   operation   in   Punjab.

Fallacy IV: Talibans are the Pashtun's business. They are also infiltrating   in   Punjab.

Reality: The thought, factories and business of Islamic extremism is Punjab based from where it infiltrate into rest of Pakistan, South Asia   and   the   world.

Besides, some civil society alliances on peace and governance have been used for the agenda of creating new provinces in Pakistan, in which their workshops were moderated by Urdu speaking and in Abbottabad, their sessions were moderated by a Hindko speaking civil society leadership so that they may reach out a document to be shared broader in which they could claim that the demand for new provinces have come from Pakhtunkhuwa, Punjab and Sindh and equally.

Politics by the civil society leadership

There are two trends in political involvement of civil society leadership in Pakistan. Almost all of the recognized country level and provincial level leaders of the civil society actors are associated are with certain political thoughts, and majority of them is part of the political parties, and some have developed their own political parties.

Censuring names of the individuals, there level ranges from the advisors, think tanks, and central leaders of the parties of General Musharaf, Nawaz Sharif, and his brother Shahbaz Sharif, Asif Ali Zardari, Asfandyar Wali, Imran Khan, Altaf Hussain, Mehmmod Khan Achakzai, Ayaz Lateef Palijo, Dr. Qadir Magsi; Mehmood Khan Achakzai, Dr. Hai Baloch, Dr. Malik Baloch, and Mir Hasil Khan Bizanjo. Out of them, ethnic Punjabi, Urdu, and Hindko speaking are well connected with the Pakistan's security establishment; a few Sindhis are also at the outer level of engagement with the security agencies.

The civil society leadership of Sindh and Balochistan that have dissent with the establishment, are against the military's anti-people role, and are critics of the security establishment that supports extremism. Hence, they are discouraged, unemployed, persecuted, and trapped through the existing top level or second tier leadership of the civil society in Pakistan.

The case of Omar Asghar Khan, who dissented General Musharaf, Asim Akhund, who refused to work for ISI's Russian section, Hassan Dars, who kept on inspiring the Sindh youth, Nausheen Qambrani who was an inspiration and vocal civil society leadership for Balochistan and myself in Sindh prey victim of them. Out of these known cases to me, Nausheen Qambrani, a mother of one child, has survived the persecution and I am still alive after the murder attempts in Pakistan, Nepal and India. It is worth mentioning here that Ms. Qambrani was persecuted only because she logistically facilitated a Canadian mission that wanted to support Baloch War IDPs (Internally Displaced Persons).

Compromises by Pakistani civil society

The level of compromises by Pakistani civil society leadership is astonishing. Once I sent an email to Asma Jahangir and CC'd to a couple of seniors and friends like Mr. Karamat Ali and Mohammad Tahseen while I was working with South Asia Partnership Pakistan over the issue of Zarina Mari, a Baloch girl kidnapped by Pakistan Army from Balochistan and was made sex-slave by the intelligence unit. None replied.

When talked on the phone with later two friends, I was told that they would prefer to talk about broader issues of Balochistan in the public civil society discussions but would keep mum over the Zarina Mari's issue, as it was an individual case. 'Zulfi we should keep ourselves out of this. Balochistan is an entirely different affair,' I was told by a friend.

Human Rights Commission of Pakistan's visits of Balochistan in 2009 and 2010 have proved to be astonishing. When Asma Jahangir visited Quetta, Balochistan according to an Urdu daily of Balochistan, a mother of the Baloch activist asked her for legal support for her missing young son who was kidnapped by the Pakistani intelligence agencies. She replied her, according to the newspaper; she will not forward the legal support to the persons who are killing the army men and Punjabi civilians; however, the same Asma Jahangir offered to be lawyer of Ajmal Qasab (a terrorist involved in 26/10 Mumbai mayhem) because according to her, Qasab's right to fair trial was being violated.

In my personal matter, when ISI and MI were forcedly ousting me from Pakistan, I shared this with honorable Karamat Ali of Pakistan Institute for labor Education, Research (PILER), and Mohammad Waseem of Indus Resource Centre (IRC). They were unfortunately weaker enough that they suggested me to leave country, rather staying in Pakistan and putting the life in danger.

"Hush! Do not hold press conference! This is not the proper time for these things," Karamat Ali told me when we were driving together to join the dinner with a Bangladeshi Official of the OXFAM GB, Asia Office. He also shared some similar views when we were attending the Karachi Book Festival and all of sudden were interrupted by the arrival of the Ayesha Siddiqa.

Around May 20, 2012, I was taking flight to Nepal for holding a meeting with the Kanak Mani Dixit to consult with him since a few days ago I was asked by the Pakistani establishment's seniors to quit Pakistan. Unexpectedly, Karamat Ali, Mahesh Kumar and some other journalists of Karachi and Hyderabad Press Club were about to take flight for Mumbai, India.

I took Karamat ji to a side and told him the situation and shared with him that I am leaving country. He simply replied that he would be traveling to Holland, after visiting India and would be unable to do anything regarding my issue. "While getting settled outside Pakistan, please complete the position paper on the land rights in Pakistan and send the document back to Zulfiqar Shah (not myself) of PILER," he suggested.

After returning back from Nepal (I was maneuvered tactically by ISI to return to Pakistan), another friend, and ex-senior of mine, Mohammad Tahseen was unable to do anything to save me. Similarly, Marvi Sirmad, a prominent rights activist, when was asked by the First Post reporter in India regarding my issue, she refused to know me. The facts are otherwise.

Our organization, The Institute for Social Movements, Pakistan (ISM) worked in association UNDP-SDPD led by Marvi over the larger consultation in Sindh province regarding the implementation of eighteenth constitutional amendment in Pakistan. Similarly, some Sindhi leaders of the civil society were either compromised or were pressurized enough to keep quite. Moreover, some civil society actors themselves became the sources of disinformation to the world outside Pakistan!

It is popular tit-bit of the Pakistani civil society that NGOs and the Military have commonalities. Both do not go for elections and both want the deep engagement with the people. And, at the end they are responsible not to the people, but to the superiors or the funders.

Adorable for the military

Punjab based major civil society organizations have a different culture. By mid of 2013, Imtiyaz Alam of South Asia Free Media Association (SAFMA) invited Pakistan Fisherfolk Forum leader Mohammad Ali Shah and his friends over the dinner. When both discussed the issue of controversial Kalabagh Dam, against which Sindhi have been struggling since last a couple of decades, Imtiaz

Alam asked his gunmen to point the gun on Shah and asked shah to agree with him on the issue of Kalabagh Dam.

There are two popular terms in some of the Punjab based leading civil society organizations of Pakistan. They informally call their Executive Directors as Generals, Deputy Directors as Lieutenant Generals, and Program Managers as Brigadiers.

The worst example of some Pakistani civil society's Punjabi-Urdu leaders' love for the military dictators was their support to Musharaf after his coup against Nawaz Sharif. The leading Punjabi civil society faces of Pakistan who have been traveling in South Asian countries since beyond last one decade, asked Musharaf to accommodate Omer Asghar Khan as a Minister, and he took oath under Musharaf as a Federal Minister.

One of our Sindhi senior friends from district Sanghar stitched his waste coat, to become the Governor of Sanghar, since Musharaf was planning to declare the districts of Pakistan as Provinces. In so many cases, military of Pakistan matters a lot in wining positivity for their friend civil society organizations.

How the civil society of Pakistan is militarized, Punjabized and Urduized and how Pakistani establishment easily manipulates international feel and perception and use it as a tool of disinformation is one of the worth analyzing model of the genuine mess in Pakistan! Amid such a situation, peace, rights, and civil democracy are almost impossible in Pakistan!

My apologies to my good old Pakistani civil society friends and seniors that I have shared a tiny part of our conversations, hiding the major part of these is a conscious act to keep on the good will!

Published on www.merinews.com on January 08, 2014

CLIMATE, LAND & POLITICS

Question of Land Reforms in Pakistan

The rural society and agriculture sector of Pakistan is chained by feudal relationships which have given birth to an evil land-tenure system with a high degree of land concentration, absentee landlordism, insecurity of tenure for share-croppers and low agricultural productivity. According to a report, around ten million children are doing labor in brick kilns, farms, carpet manufacturing workshops and restaurants and another twenty million workers engaged in agriculture and industry work as bonded labor. Feudalism is the real problem and all other problems strem from it. The feudal lords and their allies constitute only five per cent of our agricultural households and own 64 per cent of our farm land. The rest of the 95 per cent are only their political vote-bank.

The total land area of the country is about 803,940 square kilometers. About 48 million hectares, or 60 percent, is classified as unusable for forestry or agriculture and consists mostly of deserts, mountain and demographic settlements. About 21.9 million hectares is being cultivated. Nearly 65 per cent of the cropped area is in Punjab, perhaps 25 per cent in Sindh and 10 per cent in the NWFP and in Balochistan. Farming is Pakistan's largest economic activity.

In Punjab, tenancies are split more evenly between share and fixed rent contracts. Landlords in Punjab are much smaller than those in Sindh, with a median holding of only seven acres of land, and are more likely to be residing in the same village as their tenants. In Sindh, more than one third of the land is tenanted and about two-thirds of land is under sharecropping, a form of farming where output is shared between the landowner and tenant.

Sharecropping is the predominant form of tenancy in Sindh where the land ownership distribution is particularly skewed. According to a study, a median landlord in Sindh owns 28 acres of land, whereas nearly 80 per cent of the share-tenants are landless farmers. Big landlords in the province often employ kamdars to manage their tenants.

Unlike India, Pakistan did not carry out essential land reforms soon after independence and has, as a result, failed to facilitate the much-needed transition of productive relations from feudal-agrarian stage to industrial one. However, three isolated attempts were made to reduce landholdings at intervals but these could not bring feudal system to an end. In the early 1950s, provincial governments attempted to eliminate some of the absentee landlords or rent collectors, but they had little success in the face of strong opposition.

In January 1959, General Ayub Khan's government issued land reform regulations that aimed 'to boost agricultural output, promote social justice, and ensure security of tenure.' A ceiling of about 200 hectares of irrigated land and 400 hectares of non-irrigated land was placed on individual ownership; compensation was paid to owners for land surrendered. Numerous exemptions, including title transfers to family members, dampened the impact of the ceilings. Slightly fewer than one million hectares of land were surrendered, of which a little more than 250,000 hectares were sold to about 50,000 tenants. The land reforms failed to lessen the power or privileges of the landed elite.

In March 1972, the Z. A. Bhutto government announced further land reform measures, which went into effect in 1973. The landownership ceiling was lowered to about five hectares of irrigated land and about twelve hectares of non-irrigated land; exceptions were limited to an additional 20 per cent of land for owners having tractors and tube wells. The ceiling could also be extended for poor-quality land. The owners of confiscated land received no compensation, and beneficiaries were not charged for land distributed.

Official statistics showed that by 1977 only about 520,000 hectares had been surrendered, and nearly 285,000 hectares had been redistributed among about 71,000 farmers. The 1973 measure required landlords to pay all taxes, water charges, seed costs, and one-half of the cost of fertilizer and other inputs. It prohibited eviction of tenants as long as they cultivated the land, and it gave tenants first rights of purchase. Other regulations increased tenants' security of tenure and prescribed lower rent rates than had existed.

The ceilings on private ownership of farmland in 1977 were further reduced to about four hectares of irrigated land and about eight hectares of non-irrigated land. Besides, agricultural income became taxable but small farmers owning ten hectares or fewer were exempted. The military regime of Zia ul-Haq did not make efforts to implement these reforms. Governments in the 1980s and early 1990s avoided any significant attempt at strict implementation of the land reform measures, because they got much of their support from landed aristocracy of the country.

Agrarian reforms in Pakistan have never transformed rural society in the context of property structure and production relations. The limits in reforms were fixed in terms of the individual but not family holdings, which resulted in transfer of land to family members and relatives. In times of the military rule, feudal lords support the ruling junta to protect their system. And the military badly needs them.

Even after three waves of land reforms, 3,529 Zamindars have 5, 13,114 holdings of more than 100 acres in the irrigated areas, and 3, 32,273 holdings exceeding 100 acres in un-irrigated areas. Some 7, 94,774 Khatedars have 54, 64,771 land holdings of less than 12 acres in irrigated areas. In un-irrigated areas 1, 44,098 are reported to have 16, 28,826 holdings of less than 24 acres.

Land reforms play an important role in reducing poverty and empowering the poor farmers. In Pakistan, the power of landed aristocracy has acted as a barrier to social and economic progress of the rural society. Genuine land reform can help solve the problems caused by the fact that farmers often use relatively inefficient capital-intensive techniques due to distorted market prices and that small farmers do not have access to the liberal credit subsidies on imported machinery and capital equipment.

Under any scheme of serious reforms, the land ceiling should be fixed at 50 acres irrigated and 100 acres non-irrigated land. The necessary legislation should be done in favor of land reforms and Haq-e-Shifa. All laws and regulations regarding land developed under colonial era need to be abandoned and a judicial commission on land utilization should be formed to check exceeding commercialization of land. Under Haq-e-shifa, the agriculture land of about 8 acres should be allotted to the landless agriculture workers and peasants' families. The agriculture land occupied by or allotted to military forms and government departments should be revoked and distributed among the landless peasants under the principle of Haq-e-shifa.

Corporate forming should not be promoted. Allotment of forest land to the influential persons has to be revoked and re-allotted to the peasants on the condition of re-forestation. The occupied surveyed or un-surveyed lands in Kacho, Kaachho, Kohistan, Kach, Bailpat, Thar, Thal and elsewhere in the country must be re-surveyed and distributed among the landless peasants and agriculture workers families.

Equitable distribution at the tail-end is imperative. It is necessary that all disputed irrigation projects including Kalabagh dam are given up and water requirements of Indus Delta fully met. To avoid water logging and salinity, the canals, branches and watercourses should be lined. The government must draw up an agriculture policy with the consultation of agriculture scientists, peasants, agriculture workers and growers.

The parliament should be persuaded to pass legislation for protection of the peasant's rights, allowing them to have their trade unions, ensuring social justice and providing old age benefits to them.

Published in Daily Dawn, Pakistan on February 02, 2008

Changing Climate Poses Threat of Major Conflicts within Pakistan

The impact of changing climate in Pakistan exhibits symptoms of increase in the number of extremists' sanctuaries, wars between Sindh and Punjab, mass migrations, rise in urban violence and vote-bank loss for liberal parties.

Pakistan is tossing between floods and droughts. The ecological and socio-economic catastrophe has turned the country, especially Sindh province into a microcosm of global climate change. Accompanying social metabolism, massive displacements and the worst humanitarian crisis, the scenario offers a new conflict paradigm in the violence-hit country.

Sindh is undergoing a social upheaval, not just the change. Northern Sindh once again after ninety years had the highest temperature of the Asia, 53.5 °C recorded on May 26, 2010; which earlier was recorded at 52.8 °C on June 12, 1919.

The land of lower Indus river basin has an average temperature of 46 °C and 2 °C, with dry weather of an average 7 inches rain. Indus floods were a great source of agriculture economy in the rain deficit province but commissioning of dams and construction of water diversion canals in Punjab province has left Sindh water scarce during last two decades. Heavy rain and floods in 2010 -11 were exceptions.

The cultivation patterns have changed over the last three decades featuring a month-long delay in the crop cycle; weather extremes; squeezed autumns and springs; and erratic as well as unpredictable rainfall patterns. Almost 30% to 50 % yield decline due to an average 40% water table decline combined with 40% to 60% increase in the use of fertilizers and pesticides has devastated economy of the province. Besides, the decline in grass vegetation and thus in livestock has served not only a severe blow to the economy but to the traditional nutrition and dietary as well.

Biodiversity threats have challenged ecological balance, economical and agronomic fabric, and folk culture. In coastal Sindh, the excessive appearance of vipers and other serpents predicted flooding a few decades ago indicating communities to take precaution. Communities cannot predict anymore.

Oil rich coastal district Badin is one example. According to 1970-2000 data of Sindh Government, cultivatable land in the district decreased by one thousand hectares during 1997-98 marking 0.23 decline in per person cultivation ratio in two decades. The inland fish production marked a decline of 9.3% by 1997. The forest output value decreased by 38.6% and the loss valued at millions of dollars. The economic value of loss due to sea intrusion in the Indus Delta estimated by the experts is $ 120 million yearly.

Migration toward urban areas is increasing because of flood disasters in last two years, and will further increase if drought hits this year again. A major social transformation in rural Sindh with increasing migrations is unavoidable during the ongoing decade, which may further destabilize the feudal power bases in the province. This will eventually threaten the vote bank of popular political parties like Pakistan People's Party (PPP) and Pakistan Muslim League – Functional (PML - F). Meanwhile, the emerging ethnic Sindhi trader, salaried and semi-urban middle class have posed threats to the vote cordon as well as street dominance of Mutahida Qaumi Movement (MQM) in Karachi, which may translate into the rise in the urban violence.

If these climate change patterns keep exhibiting the floods and droughts like situation, a humanitarian crisis of another kind will emerge. During last two years of flood disaster, a considerable number of IDP (internally displaced population) youths from the north Sindh were reported to be recruited by the Taliban in lieu of remuneration for their families. Besides, various religious outfits including Jamaa't-ud-Dawa on the promise of ration and other humanitarian support converted nearly 1000 Dalit families in South Sindh, particularly in Badin district. If changing climate patterns create a drought like situation in Thar Desert in Sindh, more conversions and migration can be foreseen in the province.

As predicted by the climate change modulated predictions by IPCC, Punjab province will follow acute dryness in the upcoming decades, which eventually will increase the population pressure on Sindh and may give birth to the water wars and ethnic violence based on demographic securities and concerns between both of the provinces.

Coping with the climate change challenges, Pakistan needs to declare an environmental emergency. It also needs a visionary governance based on the long-term planning about agriculture, livestock, and fisheries; urbanization and rural development; institutional reorientation, and water as well as disaster management.

Essential would be the climate research in the fields of agriculture, irrigation, livestock, fisheries, and food security combined by the legislation for water, forest, agriculture, shores and coastline and environment at federal and provincial levels.

Government of Sindh needs to set up a scientific and research authority on climate change and researchers from across the world should be provided with the necessary trainings. A Center of Excellence in the Climate Change Studies at the University of Sindh would be the best serving initiatives. Climate Change should also be included as a learning unit in secondary textbooks.

Published on www.merinews.com on August 24, 2012

Political Economy of Climate Change in Pakistan

Climate change has left a devastative impact on the Sindh province of Pakistan, posing threats to its economic, social and security fabric. The scenario contains possibilities of worst long-lasting changes in the demography, ethnic security, life, and livelihood. More than 20 million people have already been displaced along with the loss of hundreds of billion dollars during the 2010-2011 floods. This is just a beginning of the climate theatre.

Subtropical Sindh temperature averages fall between 46 °C and 2 °C. It has dry weather, although it receives rainfall from two systems – the westerly monsoon from the Bay of Bengal in the Indian Ocean and the easterly rain system from the Himalayan northeast.

The water requirement of Sindh has historically been fulfilled by the Indus floods. The last two decades were extremely dry due to scarce raining coupled with insufficient water discharge to the downstream Indus. Such a reduced flow was manmade because of 'water-theft' by the upper riparian Punjab province through dams and water diversions channels. The situation kicked off an extensive ecological disaster in the Indus Delta region of the lower riparian Sindh. The Indus flood of 2010 and rain floods of 2011 were not only the exceptions due to the changing climate patterns but also a shock to the people who had been experiencing dryness and water scarcity for two decades, and thus, were unprepared for the suddenly changed situation and consequently, thrown into heavy humanitarian crises.

Northern Sindh, the passage of the thermal equator, has extreme dry features. The highest temperature ever recorded in Sindh was

53.5 °C at the archeological site of Mohen-jo-Daro on 26 May 2010, which was the fourth highest temperature on the earth; however this preceded the second highest of the region 52.8 °C, which was also recorded in Sindh on June 12, 1919. Above 6,800 feet altitude, in the hill peaks of Kirthar temperatures mostly fall below the freezing point during December – January; however, at the Indus plains, it occasionally drops to 0 °C and once every 25 years it falls to −7 °C.

The globally changing climate has left more catastrophic impacts on Sindh than on any coastal area of South Asia. A remarkable change in the precipitation levels has been noted during 1970-2000, indicating above 9% annual increase in the southeastern parts of the province, above 70% increase in the northern parts, and a decline of 32% to 38% in Southwestern Sindh.

According to a research study conducted by the author for Inter Church Organization for Development Coordination (ICCO) - Netherlands, the cultivation cycle as well as patterns change has debased the traditional agriculture calendar of the region, as the cropping calendar has now forwarded one month ahead. Increase in weather extremes coupled with the shortened autumns and springs; and undergoing erratic and unpredictable rainfall patterns has capsized living style, culture, and agriculture economy. A decreasing water table by 30% to 40% combined with soil degradation has caused a decline of 30% to 50% yield reduction in various crop pattern areas, although the use of agriculture inputs has increased over last two decades from 40% to 60%. Besides, reduction in the grass cover has caused decline in the quantity of livestock, which along with other factors like the dairy industry has caused a hike in dairy products. The impacts of changing climate have started altering social chemistry of the province.

Subsoil water table in the province stabilizes only during the exceptional floods and rainfalls. Cold weather intensity has perceptibly increased across the province; however, its duration has now become confined to an average period of one month, which earlier went on for two to three months.

Biodiversity impacts of the climate change are visible through reduction of many species and the extinction of some. Rare species like jungle cats, tigers, wolves, jackals, gazelle and deer are almost extinct and herons, doves, ducks, grey and black partridges, waterfowls, peacocks, vultures, wild boars, deer and ibexes have decreased in numbers. Balm (populus euphratica), Siras (mimosa sivissa), and Pipal (ficus religiosa) are near to extinction, while Kandi (prosopis specigera), Babul (acacia arabica), and *Kahu* coverage has reduced. Insects like butterflies are near to extinction, meanwhile the reptiles like Cobra and Gharial (gavialis gangeticus), lizards, and vipers are soon to vanish.

According to a research study on Climate Change carried out by the Oxfam GB - Pakistan, some traditional practices that were used to predict incoming sea storms and intense rainfall were the appearance of small bubbles in creek water, a bull let loose that then ran east, and seawater becoming cold. Communities would rely on these indicators to prepare themselves for intense storms. Now, however, they find that such indicators do not always manifest themselves and leave the communities unable to predict and prepare for changes in the weather.

During 1970 -2000, an extensive sea intrusion was reported in the Indus Delta area that intruded upon nearly 2 million acres land. According to a study, approximately 158,000-acre cover of Mangrove forest turned into barren plains during the mentioned period—an area that catered almost 120,000 people of the Indus Delta area with fuel wood, gave fodder support to 16,000 camels and nurtured 44 fish species. The fish and shellfish catch from the Indus Delta was 348,689 metric tons in 1993 and was reduced to 64,400 metric tons in 2000 according to the Sindh Government. Fish, prawn, and lobster catches in the lakes of coastal Badin have shrunk due to sea intrusion.

The climate change impacts on Sindh potentially turn it into a climate devastation zone of South Asia, with four major social, economic, and political dimensions:

Migrations from rural Sindh to the urban hubs of Karachi, Hyderabad, and Sukkur put huge population pressure on cities that have inadequate infrastructure. In the case of Karachi, it may give birth to ethnic conflicts and riots in the already violence-ridden metropolitan. Besides, as expected according to the modulated predictions by International Panel on Climate Change (IPCC), the remarkable decline in the rainfall and increase in the dryness in Punjab during upcoming decades most possibly increases Sindh-ward migration from Punjab, which ultimately will cause a violent conflict between Sindh and Punjab within the federation of Pakistan. In the given situation, the ongoing forced exodus of Hindus from Sindh can also be seen in the future demographic interests of Punjab province in Pakistan. There may also be an increase in the interstate migrations towards India, Iran, and Afghanistan.

The rural economy of Sindh will certainly face a huge decline, giving rise to vulnerable poverty and thereby altering the socioeconomic chemistry of the Sindhi-speaking majority.

The feudal base of power will be reduced and a sociological anarchy caused by the climate change may take place by next decade combined by a large-scale displacement.

Demographic changes in Sindh caused by decline in rural economy, reduction in agriculture output and displacements due to unpredictable Indus River and rain floods will leave deeper impacts on the political fabric of Sindh as well as Pakistan. Sharpened political conflicts along with a new political discourse will emerge containing both violent as well as reconciliatory aptitudes at the same time.

The situation will challenge governance as well as the federal practices in the country. The concerns of provincial sovereignty of Sindh and Sindhi people will extensively emerge along with the entirely new paradigm of ethnic and demographic security in Pakistan. The ongoing water conflicts in Pakistan may convert into water wars between Sindh and Punjab province and may translate into ethnic violence between Sindhis and Punjabis.

The situation may have many adverse tendencies including water rights conflicts, food insecurities, IDPs rights issues, anarchy and state failure. The scenario requires a wider range of initiatives at the Sindh regional level combined with tangible actions at the federal level:

1. An extensive process of research regarding agriculture extension services, crop patterns, harvesting, seeds and soil as well as livestock and fisheries need be undertaken.

2. Futuristic thinking over the utilization of rainwater and various sustainable irrigation methods need to be adopted.

3. Pakistan needs to declare a Climate Emergency in Sindh, which may ultimately lead to new legal and policy framework through legislation that may include the framing of:

a) Pakistan Water Act for sustainable and judicious use and interprovincial distribution of water; b) Sindh Water Act for the judicious and sustainable use and distribution of water between upper and lower riparian; c) Sindh Forrest Act for the forest preservation and reforestation and resisting all kinds of forest land grabbing;

d) Pakistan Coastal and Sindh Shore Acts for sustainable costal livelihood regime;

e) Pakistan Climate Change Act for long-term environmental policy integrated with the climate change situation; and finally; f) Sindh Building Act for the disaster resistant construction and infrastructure development.

4. An entirely new course of water management is required with special focus on the water preservations for dry seasons; water loss reduction; water treatment planning; improving water infrastructure; conservation of aquifer and water bodies as well as flood water utilization planning.

5. A new framework of disaster management needs to be placed at federal, provincial and community levels based on minimizing tube well irrigation, eradicating illegal private structures near the riverbanks, disaster mitigation planning, fodder preservation planning during the floods, and improved flood management.

6. Research bodies and institution focused on the climate change be established at federal and Sindh level and their coordination mechanism must be developed. The experts, scientists, and researchers should be provided with the necessary scientific training and access to the climate data.

7. Political parties, parliamentarians and bureaucracy should be often briefed on the climate change.

Published on Atlantic Community, Germany in 2012 www.atlantic-community.org

www.ingramcontent.com/pod-product-compliance
Lightning Source LLC
Chambersburg PA
CBHW050445290526
45786CB00006B/2164